Marked
by the
Anointing

The Process by Which the
Holy Spirit Empowers Ordinary
Men for Extraordinary Work

Anthony Trezza

WESTBOW
PRESS®
A DIVISION OF THOMAS NELSON
& ZONDERVAN

WestBow Press books may be ordered through booksellers or by contacting:

WestBow Press
A Division of Thomas Nelson & Zondervan
1663 Liberty Drive
Bloomington, IN 47403
www.westbowpress.com
844-714-3454

Because of the dynamic nature of the Internet, any web addresses or links contained in this book may have changed since publication and may no longer be valid. The views expressed in this work are solely those of the author and do not necessarily reflect the views of the publisher, and the publisher hereby disclaims any responsibility for them.

Any people depicted in stock imagery provided by Getty Images are models, and such images are being used for illustrative purposes only. Certain stock imagery © Getty Images.

Scripture taken from the NEW AMERICAN STANDARD BIBLE®, Copyright © 1960,1962,1963,1968,1971,1972,1973,1975,1977,1995 by The Lockman Foundation. Used by permission. www.Lockman.org"

Scripture taken from the King James Version of the Bible.

Scripture taken from the New King James Version® Copyright © 1982 by Thomas Nelson. Used by permission. All rights reserved.

Scripture taken from the Amplified Bible, Copyright © 1954, 1958, 1962, 1964, 1965, 1987 by The Lockman Foundation. Used with permission.

Scripture quotations taken from The Holy Bible, New International Version® NIV® Copyright © 1973 1978 1984 2011 by Biblica, Inc. TM. Used by permission. All rights reserved worldwide.

ISBN: 978-1-6642-0974-9 (sc)
ISBN: 978-1-6642-0975-6 (hc)
ISBN: 978-1-6642-0973-2 (e)

Library of Congress Control Number: 2020920726

Print information available on the last page.

WestBow Press rev. date: 11/06/2020

Acknowledgements

I would like to extend my deepest gratitude and sincerest thanks to the wonderful men and women of God who have encouraged me so greatly in the writing of this book.

To my beautiful wife of over Forty Years, Linda Lee, whose love for the Lord and deep sensitivity to the Holy Spirit has been such a great strength and encouragement to me over the years, thank you so very much for loving me and believing in me as you do.

I would also like to take this opportunity to share my love and appreciation for one of the greatest men of God I ever met, and whose anointing I drew such strength and wisdom from, Apostle Tom McGuinness, my Pastor, who I served for over 34 years and who has since gone home to his reward. I would also like to thank his anointed wife, Pastor Liz McGuinness, who has been like a mother to me.

To Pastor Mark Gorman, who after hearing this revelation was the first to encourage me to write this book, and who has since preached this revelation all over the world. Thank you, Pastor Mark, for all your help and encouragement, may the Lord bless you richly.

To Pastor Tommy Holohan, a teachers teacher, who after reading this book, declared Marked by the Anointing, a must read for any serious Christian and a revelation that should be taught in bible colleges around the world, thank you for your encouraging words.

Finally, I would like to extend my sincerest appreciation to my pastor, Kevin McGuiness, a preachers preacher, and a great man of faith, who has encouraged and supported me greatly in getting this book released to the church. Thank you for standing with me.

Foreword

By
Pastor Mark Gorman
Grace Christian Center of New Orleans

It has been several years since I first heard Pastor Anthony Trezza, a dear friend, preaching something which flipped some of my theology "on its ear"! I was the son of a man who had led a church of 100 people, in New Orleans, to grow to more than 6,000. He had a live, daily 1-hour TV program seen in all 50 states and other countries. It was necessary for 6 church services each Sunday to contain the crowds of people coming to see and experience the numerous miracles God performed through my dad's ministry. In addition, every week there was a Monday Night Miracle Rally. This was attended regularly by people from 3 states away, driving more than 200 miles each way, just to experience what God was doing at our church each week.

When you grow up in that type of environment, there is a tendency to begin to think that you've "seen it all", if you know what I mean. Obviously, that was pride, but living in that environment, of constant Revival, you tend to begin to think you know more than you know. So, when I heard Anthony redefining a word, I'd heard my entire life, saying that it didn't mean what I thought it meant, it came as quite a shock. Especially when I realized that he had done all his research, as he always does. He was telling me, for the first time, the actual meaning of the word, "anointing".

Everything I thought I knew for all those years was suddenly turned upside down. I sat and received a major education from a man my age. He did not grow up with a father who pastored a large church. He did not see blind eyes and deaf ears opened, people get out of wheelchairs on a regular basis, his entire childhood. No, Anthony received this revelation, not from someone else's book, TV program or website. He received it by bathing his ministry in prayer, diligently studying, and researching the Word of God, and then preaching what God revealed to him, with no hint of pride or arrogance. He "studied to show himself approved unto God, a workman who needed not to be ashamed, rightly dividing the Word of Truth". That day, my theology was transformed, as I learned at the feet of Pastor Anthony Trezza.

PREFACE

Some years ago, while driving in my car, I was listening to a minister on Christian radio that was using the word "anointing" quite a bit in his message. I was familiar with the word, having heard it many times before. At first, I did not give it much thought. But then something happened, I found myself asking the Lord, "what is the anointing? I hear it mentioned so often, but not with any real clarity as to what it is. What is it?"

I do not know if I was expecting Him to answer; I just found myself with a really strong desire to comprehend what the anointing was. The Lord did answer, and His answer was not at all what I was expecting to hear. He responded to my question with an instruction. He said, "I want you to teach My people about the anointing." "How can I teach Your people about the anointing when I don't know what it is?" I replied. His response, "I will teach you and you will teach them."

This book is the result of the Lord teaching me about the anointing, my effort to obey His direction, and a sincere desire to share it with you. It is not my intention to bring correction to anyone, or to appear condescending in any way. I say this, knowing full well that this revelation may challenge many of us to reconsider the way we have been applying the word "anointing" in our messages, in our prayers, and in our everyday conversation.

CONTENTS

Chapter 1

Understanding the Anointing

IN THESE MODERN times, much of how the anointing is understood and applied by the church has little if any biblical roots to draw from. Today, when many in the church speak about the anointing, or believe they are experiencing the anointing, what they are really referring to is the operation of the Holy Spirit. The first truth we must accept if we are to understand the anointing is this: **the anointing is not a power; it is the process through which the Holy Spirit operates through mortal man.** Therefore, the ability to distinguish between the operation of the Holy Spirit and the purpose of the anointing is paramount to understanding how to function effectively within the anointing.

Today, it is quite common to hear such phrases as, "more anointing," "fresh anointing," "feel the anointing," "double portion of the anointing," "anointing fall on me." These sayings may sound nice, but they cannot be traced to the Bible. The truth is, you can search the Bible from cover to cover and you will never find the anointing referred to in any of the ways I just mentioned.

Yet these statements, and many more just like them, have become accepted doctrine within the modern-day church. You may be interested to know that no one in the Bible, not even in the Book of Acts, referred to the anointing the way many in the church do today. As we progress through this book, we will look at what the scriptures actually do say and compare that to what has become the current accepted doctrine regarding the anointing.

There are significant truths we need to know about the anointing if we are going to operate in it according to God's will. For instance, the Bible only declares that you either are, or are not, anointed. The Word of God says nothing about you being more or less anointed. Therefore, a double portion of the anointing has no Biblical relevance. And since the anointing never gets stale, it never needs to be made fresh again, so there is no need for a fresh anointing. Also, there is not one single account in the entire Word of God where anyone ever said they felt the anointing, though it is filled with accounts of people operating in it. And you can read the Bible from Genesis to Revelation and not find one account where the anointing ever fell on anyone, yet it is filled with examples of the Holy Spirit falling on the anointed. And since the anointing is permanent, you cannot find one Biblical account of it ever lifting off anyone as if it comes and goes.

Am I suggesting that we can no longer say such things? Honestly, I do not think it is an issue if we do. But these statements, and many more just like them, lead believers to pray unscriptural and inaccurate prayers by making them think what they need is one thing when what they are really looking for is another.

The Lord wills that all New Covenant believers be witnesses of His power by demonstrating His power. This is absolute truth. This is His will for all believers. However, according to the Bible, the only way the Holy Spirit will release His power through a vessel of flesh is through the anointing. Yet, the anointing remains one of the most misunderstood and misquoted topics in all of Christendom.

The anointing is such a vital principle in the Kingdom of God that Moses was commanded by the Lord that before any man or vessel could be put into service they must first be anointed. This same order of, **"anointing, before power"**, holds just as true for the New Covenant church. It is therefore of great significance to the advancement of the kingdom of God, especially in these times of such darkness, that we come to the true Biblical understanding on this most important of topics. **Know this: The Holy Spirit will only work through an anointed vessel.**

When you understand what the "anointing" really is, and begin to operate in it, you will never again fail to see the power of God manifest through you. That is a big claim. Yet, it is the absolute truth. Nowhere in the Word of God will you ever find an account of anyone who was anointed, and **walking in obedience to God,** failing to accomplish that which they were anointed to do, nowhere.

The Anointing Defined

The word translated anointing in the Old Testament is *Mashah*, which simply means **to smear.** In the Bible we see that this was accomplished by the act of either rubbing or pouring the anointing oil upon the object or person being anointed. **The Anointing was the result of being smeared with oil.**

The word translated anointing in the New Testament is *Chrio,* which is always a symbolic smearing, not an actual smearing with oil as in the Old Covenant. This is because in the New Covenant we are anointed with the Holy Spirit, not with oil. Again, just as in the Old Covenant, **the Anointing is the result of being anointed.**

It is extremely important to understand that there are a few substantial differences in how the anointing operates in the New Covenant compared to how it operated in the Old Covenant. One of the biggest differences is that in the Old Covenant, one was anointed with oil, a type of the Holy Spirit, whereas in the New Covenant, one is anointed with the Holy Spirit. There are no more types and shadows in the New Covenant. The other big difference is that in the Old Covenant only a select few were anointed, whereas in the New Covenant, all Born Again believers are anointed. What does remain the same in both covenants is that the "anointing" is the result of someone being "anointed".

You must realize that no matter how misunderstood the anointing is in this modern age, it was no great mystery back in Biblical times. As a matter of fact, the practice of anointing people and objects was just as common back then as the acts of spreading or smearing are today. Back in the days of the Bible if someone were smearing butter on their bread, they would say they were anointing their bread with butter. However, when the process of anointing was used in the kingdom of God, it indicated that someone or something was now marked and set apart for a specific service to the Lord.

We are at a real disadvantage in these modern times regarding our ability to comprehend the true meaning of the words which so powerfully describe our salvation. Words we use constantly in our services, messages, teachings, and everyday conversations as Christians, are so often misunderstood and misinterpreted by sincere believers. *Anointing, Grace, Redemption, Justification,* and even *Salvation*, were all common everyday words which had real meaning to the people of those times. Therefore, when God used these words and others like them to teach and define His kingdom, the early church knew full well what God was saying. In this day and time these words have become almost completely exclusive to the church. As a result of us not being acquainted with the original use of these words, we as the church have somehow redefined them. There may be no greater example of this than with the word, **"anointing"**.

There were two different words used in the New Testament that were both translated as anointing. The first, *Chrio*, was always limited in its use to the sacred and symbolical anointings which, as we mentioned earlier, refer to the anointing of the Holy Spirit. The other word translated anointing in the New Testament, and the one which is used most frequently, is *Aleipho*, which simply means **to smear with oil or ointment**. This word for anointing was always used when referring to the cultural practice of anointing.

The cultural practice of anointing was quite common back in

Biblical times. Anointing the face or body with oil was a largely accepted and widespread practice among ancient middle eastern cultures. People would regularly smear oil on their bodies and faces to protect the skin from the harsh elements of the climate. They referred to this practice as anointing themselves. The act of anointing people was also observed when someone wanted to honor an important guest or to prepare a body for burial.

In this book, we will be dealing with the anointing of the Holy Spirit. There is a very real difference between the cultural practice of anointing, and the anointing of the Holy Spirit. Not understanding this can, and often does, lead to confusion. The cultural practice of anointing is mentioned frequently throughout the Old and New Testaments; you can see it in everything from ceremonially anointing kings into office to anointing the sick with oil.

> *Is anyone among you sick? Let him call for the elders of the church, and let them pray over him, anointing him with oil in the name of the Lord; 15 and the prayer offered in faith will restore the one who is sick, and the Lord will raise him up,...*
> **James 5:14-15** NASB

Notice, it is not the anointing with oil that heals the sick. It is, and always has been, the prayer of faith that heals the sick. We must be careful to not mix the cultural aspects of anointing with the powerful properties uniquely associated with the anointing of the Holy Spirit. Much of what the modern church attributes to, and uses anointing oil for, actually finds its origins in the **cultural aspects of anointing,** *(Aleipho),* rather than the **anointing of the Holy Spirit,** *(Chrio).*

The setting apart for His service and the endowment of special abilities, which are all part of the anointing of the Holy Spirit, is what we will be addressing in this book.

5

The Process of the Anointing of the Holy Spirit

Anoint: The **marking** and **setting apart** of someone for a particular service.

Anointed: The **result** of being marked and set apart for service.

Anointing: Encompasses the entire process. It is an all-inclusive word that covers everything from **"to anoint"**, the resulting effect which is to be **"anointed"**, and the operation and special endowments of the Holy Spirit that work through those who are anointed.

In the Old Covenant - Anointing was always connected with the oil that was used to anoint. So, in the Old Covenant, the anointing referred to being anointed with oil and the resulting endowments and power which accompanied that.

In the New Covenant - We are not anointed with oil. We are anointed with the Holy Spirit, and the One who anoints us, is Jesus Christ Himself.

1 John 2:20

20 But you have an anointing from the Holy One, ... NASB

The **Holy One,** that we have an anointing from, is Jesus. He is the One referred to as the **"Holy One"** in the Word of God. (Psalm 16:10; Isaiah 10:20; Isaiah 43:14; Habakkuk 1:12; Mark 1:24; Acts 2:27; Acts 3:14; Acts 13:35; Rev 3:7).

The Anointing is Not the Holy Spirit

1 John 2:20
20 But you have an anointing from the Holy One, ...

Do you see where it says, *"...you have "an" anointing..."*? The Apostle John is referring to a particular anointing that we have as believers. We will discuss this anointing later on in the book in the chapter titled, **The Two Anointing's of the Believer.** Since there are many anointings, and John was referring to a particular one, he used the wording, *"... you have "an" anointing..."*. He cannot possibly be referring to the Holy Spirit because there is only one Holy Spirit.

So, even though the anointing contains the operation of the Holy Spirit, it is not the Holy Spirit. This is important to know because there is some confusion in the church regarding this. For instance, throughout the entire Book of Acts, the church always credits the operating of miracles to the Holy Spirit, not the anointing. Whereas in the modern-day church, many give credit to the anointing and not the Holy Spirit.

Much of the accepted doctrine regarding the anointing today results from not having a clear understanding of the distinction between the anointing and the operation of the Holy Spirit. This lack of understanding produces beliefs and practices which are not found anywhere in the Bible, yet are adhered to by many in the present-day church.

We will discuss all this and more in greater detail throughout this book. However, it is necessary that we first get a clear understanding of what the Bible says so that we can better distinguish between the Biblical concept of the anointing and the modern-day concept.

Let's Go to the Beginning

To better understand the anointing the way God intended, we must go to where this process was first recorded in the Word of God. We will find this in the book of Genesis, chapter 28.

When Jacob journeyed from his father's house to go and live with his uncle Laban, he settled in to sleep in a place called, Luz. As Jacob slept, he had a dream. In this dream Jacob saw a ladder stretching from heaven to earth. He also saw angels ascending and descending on this ladder with the Lord standing at the top of it.

Genesis 28:16-19

> *16 Then Jacob awoke from his sleep and said, "Surely the LORD is in this place, and I did not know it." 17 And he was afraid and said, "How awesome is this place! This is none other than the house of God, and this is the gate of heaven." 18 So Jacob rose early in the morning, and took the stone that he had put under his head and set it up as a pillar, and <u>poured oil on its top</u>. 19 And he called the name of that place Bethel; however, previously the name of the city had been Luz.*
> NASB

Even though the word anointing is not mentioned at all in this account, the act of anointing is. When Jacob poured the oil upon the pillar, God referred to it as the pillar being anointed. We can see this when God recalls this event in Genesis 31:13.

Genesis 31:13

> *13'I am the God of Bethel, where you anointed a pillar, ...* NASB

When Jacob poured the oil upon the pillar, he anointed the pillar. In this introduction to the anointing we see four very distinct principles of the anointing which remain consistent throughout the entire Word of God. These four principles remain in effect throughout the Bible whenever the anointing is present.

1. **Jacob noticed there was something SPECIAL about this place.**
   In the eyes of the Lord, everyone who is anointed is special and unique and He sees something in them He wants to use. **It is the Lord who chooses who to anoint and what to anoint them for.**

2. **The place was HONORED.**
   By setting up the pillar, Jacob honored this ground as a place of significant importance. The Lord always places honor upon His anointed, and He requires that His people give honor to whom honor is due.

3. **The place was ANOINTED.**
   When Jacob anointed the pillar, he marked and set this place apart from all other places. The Lord anoints those whom He chooses, marking them and setting them apart for His special use.

4. **The place was given a PURPOSE.**
   By naming the place, Jacob gave it a purpose. Biblically, a name always has meaning and a purpose. In this case, Jacob named the place Bethel, which means, "House of God." Everyone that is anointed by the Lord is anointed for a specific purpose; and whatever they are anointed to do, the Holy Spirit will empower them to do it.

If we are to minister effectively in the anointing as the Bible clearly indicates we should, then we need to learn how to operate in it the scriptural way, and not just a traditional way. The scriptures show us that when one is anointed, they are now marked and set apart for service and are no longer common with the world around them.

CHAPTER 2

Marked and Set Apart- No Longer Common

THE ANOINTING SEPARATES you from ordinary common use unto a sacred purpose. In this chapter, we will see how the Lord takes a simple thing like smearing or rubbing (anointing) and makes the ordinary extraordinary.

Exodus 30:22 Moreover the LORD spake unto Moses, saying, 23 Take thou also unto thee principal spices, of pure myrrh five hundred shekels, and of sweet cinnamon half so much, even two hundred and fifty shekels, and of sweet calamus two hundred and fifty shekels, 24 And of cassia five hundred shekels, after the shekel of the sanctuary, and of oil olive an hin: 25 And thou shalt make it an oil of holy ointment, an ointment compound after the art of the apothecary: it shall be an holy anointing oil. 26 And thou shalt anoint the tabernacle of the congregation therewith, and the ark of the testimony, 27 And the table and all his vessels, and the candlestick and his vessels, and the altar of incense, 28 And the altar of burnt offering with all his vessels, and the laver and his foot.

29 And thou shalt sanctify them, that they may be most holy: whatsoever toucheth them shall be holy. 30 And thou shalt anoint Aaron and his sons, and consecrate them, that they may minister unto me in the priest's office. 31 And thou shalt speak unto the children of Israel, saying, This shall be an holy anointing oil unto me throughout your generations. 32 Upon man's flesh shall it not be poured, neither shall ye make any other like it, after the composition of it: it is holy, and it shall be holy unto you. KJV

In the days of Moses, the surrounding nations also had altars and corresponding tools that were used in their religious practices. They had their altars, their lampstands, their tents, and their priests. This was all quite common in that day and age. In this account we see how the Lord instructed Moses to consecrate His priests and the articles that were to be used in His service by anointing them. That was because it is the process of the anointing that takes the ordinary and makes it extraordinary. Only after Moses anointed these things would they be fit for God's use. This is an absolute key in understanding the anointing- **the Holy Spirit will not use anything or anyone that is not anointed.**

What separated the altar of God from the altars of the heathen nations was not just that it was Gods altar, it was the anointing. And what separated the priests of God from the priests of the heathen nations was also the anointing. In other words, because of the anointing, the vessels in God's temple and the priests who ministered within the temple, were no longer just like all the other vessels and priests of the surrounding nations. The anointing separated them from the world around them and made them fit for the Lords use, just like it does for you and for me.

Let this sink in; the very moment Moses anointed the tabernacle and all its utensils, they were separated from their association and commonality with the world. God was now able to use them for His purpose. However, they still looked exactly as they did before they were anointed. It was the same thing with Aaron and his sons; they were not just ordinary men anymore, they were anointed. But they still looked exactly as they did before they were anointed. The same thing is true today; your anointing separates you from the ordinary and makes you extraordinarily fit for the service of the Lord, even though you still look just like your next-door neighbor. That said, get as far away as possible from people who go around looking as if their walking in the twilight zone in order to appear "anointed".

Once anointed, Aaron and his sons were now uniquely set apart and fit for their service to God. It was not anything they did or had to do; it was the process of the anointing that sanctified them for service. It was the anointing that consecrated them for use by the Holy Spirit, not any inherent abilities of their own.

This is one of the greatest revelations regarding the anointing, because this is what it means to be anointed; **it is the anointing on someone's life that declares them fit for the Holy Spirit to use them.** If you get this, it will change your thinking and it will change your life.

God has chosen the anointing as the principle vehicle in which the Kingdom of God operates through mere mortal men and women. **Know this: The power of the Kingdom of God is the Holy Spirit, and there is no other power recognized by God. The anointing is not a power, it is a process.** The anointing is the guarantee on someone's life that the Holy Spirit will empower them to do great exploits. God will not allow flesh (the power of man) to do that which can only be done by the Holy Spirit, and that is why we need the anointing. The Word of God is absolutely clear on this.

Zechariah 4:6

...Not by might, nor by power, but by my spirit, saith the LORD of hosts. KJV

Memorize this scripture and treasure it in your heart, for this scripture sheds more light on the anointing than any other scripture in the entire Word of God. Notice what it does not say; it does not say "not by might, nor by power, but by My anointing, saith the Lord". Why? Because it is the Holy Spirit who empowers us, not the anointing. **The anointing is that which defines what we are when the power of the Holy Spirit is upon us.** But the power has and always will be the Holy Spirit.

If you are anointed to be a Pastor, then you will operate as only a Pastor can when the Holy Spirit flows through you. If you are anointed as a Prophet, then you will operate as a Prophet when the Holy Spirit flows through you. Whether you are anointed as Pastor, Teacher, Prophet, or Evangelist, it is whatever you are anointed for that you will be when the Holy Spirit operates in your life. This is important and there are no exceptions; you cannot be any of these things without the Spirit of the Lord empowering you, and the Holy Spirit will not empower you unless you are anointed.

Let me give you a great example of what I am saying:

There is certainly no ministry more demanding than that of the Pastor. The care of the Lord's flock is a profoundly serious calling. A true Pastor will be driven to prayer by the shear responsibility of their office and the humble realization that without the Lord they will certainly fail. A Pastor who has somehow learned to function in his or her own strength will inevitably find themselves feeling inadequate in their service and the enemy busily attacking their sheep. They will begin to experience burn out, weariness, and loss of vision. The vibrant lively church they once pastored is now a mere shell of what it used to be. They will then be tempted to believe that they have lost their anointing and can find themselves thinking God has changed His mind and no longer wants them to pastor. Some even leave their pastoral calling and try their hand as an evangelist, while others may be tempted to resign their ministry and pass it on to someone much younger and far less experienced. They may even contemplate retirement. This is not just an example; this is an all too common reality. This is a tragedy that is happening with more and more frequency.

In cases like this it is not the anointing that is needed, it is the Spirit of God that is needed. This is not a case of losing one's anointing to pastor, it is a case of one losing their dependence upon the Holy Spirit to pastor. Thus, not only do they suffer, but also the people they have been called to minister to suffer.

This is not just limited to pastors, this applies to all ministries including minstrels, singers, choir members, elders, anyone who serves in ministry. This is the inevitable result of anyone who performs their ministry (operates in their anointing) by their own might and by their own power instead of by the Spirit of God. **The anointing is not something that comes and goes, the anointing is a matter of - you are, or you are not.**

So, spending your time trying to get more anointing, or trying to feel the anointing would be a total waste of time for someone who is already anointed. This time would be much better spent humbling one's self in the presence of the Lord and seeking His power and His strength. Because it is and always will be, *"...Not by might, nor by power, but by my spirit, saith the LORD of hosts".*

This goes for anyone who has been anointed for ministry, no matter what their calling may be. If you are anointed, your anointing is permanent, so it is not the anointing you have lost. If you are feeling powerless and ineffective you are in disobedience to Zechariah 4:6 and are suffering the unavoidable downfall associated with all who do the same.

The Kingdom of God works this way: **It is not by your might,**

it is not by your strength, it is by the Spirit of the Lord. All the anointing in the world will not change this. The Lord wants you to be hungry for the fellowship and operation of the Holy Spirit in your life, and also upon your anointing. A true man or woman of God realizes their dependence upon the Holy Spirit. They know and accept the fact that nothing significant or life changing can ever come from themselves. Unfortunately, there are far too many who think they can be of service to the Lord in their own strength. These people will never achieve anything great for the Kingdom of God, and anything they do achieve will be lost at the Judgement Seat of Christ. Do not let this be you.

The Lord has made the anointing available to all His people. He has chosen the anointing as the method by which the Holy Spirit will work through mortal man.

If you are Born Again you are anointed.

> *1 John 2:27 But the anointing which ye have received of him abideth in you…* KJV

If you are Born Again, you have the Holy Spirit.

> *Romans 8:9 But ye are not in the flesh, but in the Spirit, if so be that the Spirit of God dwell in you…* KJV

This is the easiest way to comprehend the anointing: The anointing upon an individual's life separates them from common man and draws the power of the Holy Spirit into their life, thereby equipping them for the Lords service and enabling them to do what they have been called to do. We will look into the specific anointings later on in this book. However, I believe it is especially important to encourage all believers that they are anointed. This is a vital part of our Godly heritage in Christ.

The very moment we receive God's gift of salvation we are anointed and set apart for His service. If you are a Born-Again child of God, you are anointed. Gone are the days of the Old Covenant where only the Kings, Priests and Prophets were anointed. You are now part of a Royal Priesthood. You have been saved and sanctified by the blood of Jesus Christ, and you have been anointed to operate in the power of the Holy Ghost. You received your salvation by believing, and you can only operate in this power by believing. Best of all, because you are anointed, the Holy Spirit will even enable you to believe.

> *1 John 2:27 But the anointing which ye have received of him abideth in you, and ye need not that any man <u>teach</u> you: but as the same anointing <u>teacheth</u> you of all things, and is truth, and is no lie, and even as it hath taught you, ye shall abide in him.* KJV

As a child of God, you are no longer common because you are anointed. The Holy Spirit recognizes the anointing and is ready to empower you to be a blessing to others. The anointing is what enables us, not our abilities. Because we are anointed the Holy Spirit will flow through us when we minister to others. This was true for Jesus' earthly ministry as well, just as He declared when He began His ministry.

> *Luke 4:18 The Spirit of the Lord is upon me, <u>because he hath anointed me</u>...* KJV

Why was the Spirit of the Lord upon Jesus? According to Jesus, it was because He was anointed. Because you are anointed, the Holy Spirit is now ready to work through you too. Do you believe this? You have been marked by the Holy Spirit, set apart for God's use, and made "No Longer Common."

Here are two important things to consider in your quest to understand the anointing:

1. Since you are "No Longer Common", the Holy Spirit can indwell you and enable you to be an <u>effective and powerful</u> witness for the Kingdom of God. Remember, the Holy Spirit is drawn to the anointing, so it has nothing to do with your personal abilities or lack thereof. If you are Born Again, you are anointed.
2. The devil no longer has any claim to you. The devil no longer has any right to you. You have been marked and set apart; you are anointed for God's use. You no longer have anything in common with the world or the devil. The devil has lost his claim over you. That is why you have every right, and all the authority you need, to tell the devil to back off. You are set apart unto God, you are God's property. You have the authority and right to tell the devil, "No trespassing, I am anointed, and the power of the Holy Spirit working through my anointing destroys any and every yoke you would try to place on my life."

I would like to end this chapter with a warning regarding a practice which is accepted by far too many in the church today. Take special notice of this portion of scripture we just read in the beginning of this chapter regarding the anointing oil.

> *Exodus 30:31 And thou shalt speak unto the children of Israel, saying, This shall be an holy anointing oil unto me throughout your generations.*
>
> *32 Upon man's flesh shall it not be poured, <u>neither shall ye make any other like it, after the</u>*

composition of it: it is holy, and it shall be holy unto you. KJV

There are those within the church that believe they have the exact recipe for the anointing oil mentioned here in the book of Exodus. Furthermore, they believe, and would have you believe, that their oil has some special power that no other oil has. They somehow believe that if they anoint you with this formula you will get extra ordinary miracles that the use of some other oil would not allow. This is wrong on so many levels. This is a dangerous practice and one that should not be adhered to by any church. The power of the anointing is the Holy Spirit, not the oil. So, whether you use olive oil or vegetable oil, or some secret recipe, keep this in mind, it is not the oil that has the power, it is the Holy Spirit.

If you are feeling weak or powerless in your service to the Lord and His people, it is not more anointing that you need, it is a greater infilling of the Holy Spirit that you need, because He is the power of the anointing.

CHAPTER 3

The Power of the Anointing is the Holy Spirit

MUCH OF THE confusion surrounding the anointing comes from us not having a clear definition of what the anointing actually is. Though the Old Testament sheds an incredible amount of light upon the topic of the anointing, the New Testament rarely mentions the anointing at all. This is true even though the various operations of the anointing are clearly evident throughout the entire New Testament.

It is important to understand that the overall concept of the anointing in the Old and New Covenants is the same. However, there are two big differences. In the Old Covenant only a select few were anointed. In the New Covenant all true believers are anointed. In the Old Covenant you were anointed with holy oil, a type of the Holy Spirit. In the New Covenant you are anointed with the Holy Spirit.

> *Acts 10:38*
>
> *38 "You know of Jesus of Nazareth, how God anointed Him with the Holy Spirit and with power, ...* NASB

What remains the same between both the Old and the New Covenants is that anointed vessels are separated unto God for His service, and they are precious in His sight.

There are many in the church who speak of the anointing and the Holy Spirit as if there were no distinction. But the Bible goes to great lengths to show us that there is a distinction to be made between the anointing and the Holy Spirit. This is made crystal clear in Paul's second letter to the Corinthians.

2 Cor 1:21-22

21 Now He who establishes us with you in Christ and _anointed us_ is God, 22 who _also_ sealed us and gave us the Spirit in our hearts as a pledge.
NASB

There are those who refer to the anointing as if it were the Holy Spirit; it is not. There are others who treat the anointing as if it were some life force all its own, separate from the Father, the Son, and the Holy Spirit; it is not. The anointing is the process the Lord uses to mark and consecrate an individual for use in His service. The Lord has established the anointing to be greater than, and superior to, anything the kingdom of darkness has to offer. This includes sickness, oppression, torment, addiction, or anything else the devil may use to harm and destroy Gods creation. It is the Holy Spirit that empowers the anointing, and the Holy Spirit is God, and there is simply nothing more powerful than God.

This chapter will shed a great deal of light on the subject by helping us see that the Holy Spirit is the power behind the anointing, and that anything beneficial and productive that comes from the anointing is by way of the Holy Spirit. The Unction, or the Charisma, that many speak of when referring to the anointing, is the actual endowment that one receives from being anointed for service. But the power of this endowment remains the Holy Spirit.

Acts 10:38 How God anointed Jesus of Nazareth with the Holy Ghost and with power: who went about doing good, and healing all that were oppressed of the devil; for God was with him. KJV

When people say they feel the anointing, they are actually feeling the Holy Spirit. When people declare that they sense the anointing is increasing, it is not the anointing that is increasing, it is the presence of the Holy Spirit that is increasing upon the anointing. **Without realizing it people are taking the glory away from God, because they do not know the difference between the Holy Spirit and the anointing.**

This may sound ridiculous to some of you when I tell you not to give the glory to the anointing, but think of some of the songs you have heard, or some of the messages you have heard. There are songs sung to the anointing where the request of the singer is addressed to the anointing as if it could reply. There are messages preached on the anointing as if it were a living being with a mind that could think, reason, make decisions and come to the aid of the helpless. I know you will say that when people do these things, they are actually referring to the Holy Spirit. Well, if that is the case, why not address yourself to the Holy Spirit instead of to the anointing just as the early church did all throughout the book of acts. The mind and the reasoning behind the anointing is the Holy Spirit, and when we understand this, we will give glory to whom glory is due.

The anointing is not a being, it is the method by which the Lord sets ordinary men apart for extraordinary work. Therefore, when someone is anointed, they are not ordinary. The anointed of God are supernaturally equipped to serve in His Kingdom; and if you mess with them, you are messing with God. That is why the scripture say's in Psalm 105:15 ***"Do not touch My anointed ones;..."***. Notice the scripture does not say, "Do not touch My anointing...". If the anointing was, as many saints understand it to be, then the scripture would be warning us not to touch the anointing, instead it clearly warns us not to touch the **"anointed ones"**.

Let us look at some passages of scripture in both the Old and New Testaments which plainly and clearly demonstrate that the Holy Spirit and the anointing are not one and the same. Please do not make the mistake of thinking this is petty. The church needs this understanding so that it can pray in accordance with scripture and, thereby, see the results it so desperately needs to see. If God's people perish for lack of knowledge, then you can be assured that there are prayers that do not get answered because they are unscriptural prayers; and declarations that are powerless because they, too, are unscriptural. God is bound by His word, not your interpretation of it. You shall know the truth, and the truth shall make you free.

If this bothers you, then take a moment to think on this scripture and what it is saying regarding praying according to Gods will.

1 John 5:14-15

14 And this is the confidence which we have before Him, that, if we ask anything according to His will, He hears us. 15 And if we know that He hears us in whatever we ask, we know that we have the requests which we have asked from Him. NASB

I want to show you an example of just how far removed the modern-day church has come from understanding the anointing in its true context. Using the example of Elijah and Elisha as recorded in 2 Kings 2:9, if they were living in the church today, when Elijah asked Elisha, *"what shall I do for you before I am taken from you?",* Elisha would have responded, "give me a double portion of your anointing."

How many messages have been preached and Bible studies taught on having a double portion of the anointing? Do you know what would have happened if Elisha had asked Elijah for a double portion of his anointing? Nothing! Absolutely nothing! Why? Because Elisha knew it was not a double portion of Elijah's anointing that he wanted, it was a double portion of Who gave Elijah's anointing its power, that is what he wanted.

Let us look at this account of Elijah and Elisha as it is recorded in the Word of God.

> *2 Kings 2:9 "Now it came about when they had crossed over, that Elijah said to Elisha, 'Ask what I shall do for you before I am taken from you.' And Elisha said, 'Please, let a double portion of your spirit be upon me.'"* NASB

Elisha knew full well that what he wanted was not a double portion of Elijah's anointing, because Elisha was already anointed. You see Elisha understood what the anointing was, and he also understood what it was not. If you think about it, Elisha asking Elijah for more anointing would be like a Pastor asking an Apostle to make him more Pastor. You either are or are not a Pastor. You cannot be more Pastor. However, as a Pastor, you can certainly have a greater infilling of the Holy Spirit to empower you to be more effective in your ministry.

In the Word of God whenever someone was anointed, we see that the Holy Spirit was right there to equip and empower them to fulfill whatever it was they were called to do. We see this by the scripture either making mention of the Holy Spirit by name, or by simply recording the extra-ordinary deeds of the one who was anointed.

Let us look at the Word of God and see what happened when both Saul and David were anointed as king. We will reverse the order and start with David first, then we will look at the account of Saul.

1 Samuel 16:13 "Then Samuel took the horn of oil and anointed him (David) in the midst of his brothers; and the Spirit of the Lord came mightily upon David from that day forward..." NASB

The Spirit of the Lord is the Holy Spirit, and the Holy Spirit did not show up until after David was anointed. Look at how the scripture is worded, *"... Samuel... anointed him ... and the Spirit of the Lord came mightily upon David..."*. That little word *"and"*, between anointed and the Spirit of the Lord, shows us that the scripture is talking about more than one experience. David was anointed, and then the Holy Spirit empowered him.

We see clearly that the Holy Spirit and the anointing are not one and the same. However, they do go hand in hand. David was anointed as king, and then the Holy Spirit came upon him mightily to equip him as king. This is always God's order, first the anointing, and then the power of the anointing, which is the Holy Spirit.

Now let us look at the account of Saul being anointed as king.

1 Samuel 10:1 - "Then Samuel took the flask of oil, poured it on his (Saul's) head, kissed him and said, 'has not the Lord anointed you a ruler over his inheritance?...'" NASB

In the above portion of scripture, we see Samuel anointing Saul as king. The Word of God shows us that Samuel took the flask of oil, poured it on Saul's head, kissed him and said, *"Has not the Lord anointed you ruler over his inheritance."*

Now, I want us to read 1 Samuel 10:2-6. It shows us very clearly that the Holy Spirit and the anointing are not the same. First comes the anointing, then comes the Holy Spirit, the anointing's power.

1 Samuel 10:2 - "When you go from me today, then you will find two men close to Rachel's tomb in the territory of Benjamin at Zelzah; and they will say to you, 'The donkeys which you went to look for have been found.' Now behold, your father has ceased to be concerned about the donkeys and is anxious for you, saying, 'What shall I do about my son?'" NASB

Samuel is still prophesying:

1 Samuel 10:3-6 - "Then, you will go on from there. You will come as far as the oak of Tabar and there, three men going up to God at Bethel will meet with you. One carrying three kids, another carrying three loaves of bread and another carrying a jug of wine. They will greet you and give you two loaves of bread which you will accept from their hand. Afterward, you will come to the hill of God where the Philistine garrison is and it shall be as soon as you have come there to the city, that you will meet a group of prophets coming down from the high place with harp, tambourine, flute and lyre before them and they will be prophesying. <u>Then the Spirit of the Lord will come upon you mightily...and you will be changed into another man.</u>" NASB

Now look very carefully at what happens to Saul sometime later. Now, this is a fair amount of time after Saul had been anointed by Samuel:

1 Samuel 10:10 "When they came to the hill there... the Spirit of God came upon him (Saul) mightily, ..." NASB

In these verses of scripture, we see an even more convincing example of how the Holy Spirit and the anointing are not the same. Saul was anointed in verse one, and the Holy Spirit did not come upon him until verse ten. Saul was anointed as king, and then he traveled some distance, maybe a few hours passed by, and then the Spirit of the Lord came upon him. When the Spirit of the Lord came upon him, <u>then he was changed</u>. You see in Verse 1, he was anointed, set apart and called as king. But Saul was still the same man. It was not until the Holy Spirit came upon him that he was changed into another man. It was not until the Holy Spirit came upon him that he had any power or ability as king. **So, you see, the anointing is where one is marked and set apart for a particular service, but the Holy Spirit is the power which makes the anointing work and equips the individual for that service.**

Let us look at what the New Testament says about this, and we will hear it from the greatest authority of all, Jesus Christ (Christ-The Anointed One).

Luke 4:18-"The Spirit of the Lord is upon Me, <u>because He anointed Me</u> to preach the gospel to the poor. He has sent Me to proclaim release to the captives, and recovery of sight to the blind, to set free those who are downtrodden, to proclaim the favorable year of the Lord." NASB

Jesus is quoting Isaiah 61 which talks about the anointing on the coming Messiah. Jesus was declaring that which Isaiah prophesied about Him. That is why He said after quoting Isaiah, *"Today in your hearing, this scripture has been fulfilled"*. In this account,

Jesus describes His anointing and what it will accomplish. Jesus also informs us why the Holy Spirit came upon Him.

> *Luke 4:18-"The Spirit of the Lord is upon me,*
> *<u>because</u> He anointed me..."*

This is the way the Kingdom of God operates. The Holy Spirit will not come upon you to equip you until you are first anointed. Jesus says it, **"The Spirit of the Lord is upon me..."**, for this reason, *"...Because He has anointed Me."*

Do we understand that Jesus never did a miracle in His own power? Everything He did was accomplished by the power of the Holy Spirit. He did this to be an example to us, to show us that we do not need to rely on our own power or abilities, but that we should rely upon the Holy Spirit. The only way the church of Jesus Christ is going to see the results it has been praying for is to let the Holy Spirit do what He has come to do. There is no greater example of this in the Word of God than Jesus Himself.

From the very moment He was born, Jesus was anointed. Yet, He did not perform one miracle until the Holy Spirit came upon Him. On the night He was born the angel declared, *"For unto you is born...a Savior, which is Christ the Lord"*. One of the titles the angel gave Him is Christ, from the Greek- **Christos**, translated *anointed One*. Jesus was anointed at birth. However, He performed no miracles, nor did He operate in any supernatural powers until thirty years later when the Holy Spirit came upon Him at the river Jordan.

Matthew 3:13-16

13 Then cometh Jesus from Galilee to Jordan
unto John, to be baptized of him...

16 And Jesus, when he was baptized, went up straightway out of the water: <u>and, lo, the heavens were opened unto him, and he saw the Spirit of God descending like a dove, and lighting upon him:...</u> KJV

Thirty years after the angel declared Jesus the Anointed One, the Holy Spirit came upon Him. That is when the miraculous began to occur in the life and ministry of our Lord Jesus; and not one moment before. Only after this Jordan experience was Jesus able to declare, *"The Spirit of the Lord is upon Me because He has anointed Me..."*. This is the way the Kingdom of God operates.

Look at what Jesus said regarding all believers:

"But You shall receive power <u>when</u> the Holy Spirit comes upon you..." Acts 1:8 NASB

Notice that Jesus did not say, "But you shall receive power when you are anointed". He said, "But you shall receive power when the Holy Spirit comes upon you". Jesus already anointed the disciples for ministry as recorded in *Mark 16:15-19*. But here in Acts, He gives the disciples instructions to wait until the power of their anointing showed up before beginning their ministries. Notice, He did not tell them to wait until they got their act together. He told them to wait until the power of their anointing showed up. If God has called you into His service, it is not the anointing which you are waiting for, it is the power of the anointing, the Holy Spirit, which you are waiting for.

Where is the tarrying for the Holy Spirit that once made men and women so powerful and effective in their service to God? How can someone tarry for something they do not even realize they need? Many have lost their dependency upon the Holy Spirit and spend valuable time seeking God for that which He has already supplied.

They do this because of erroneous doctrines regarding the anointing, doctrines which cannot be substantiated by the Word of God.

When Jesus told the disciples to tarry, He put the emphasis on receiving power. The Holy Spirit has been given to the present-day church for the same reason He was given to the disciples on the day of Pentecost. The reason is that we would declare the gospel of Jesus Christ in power and in demonstration of the Holy Spirit. It is time for the church to wake up and realize that we are already anointed, and that what we need is the Holy Spirit. We do not need a fresh anointing; we need a fresh outpouring of the Holy Spirit. We do not need a double portion of the anointing; we need a greater infilling of the Holy Spirit. We are already anointed. **Why do we pray for what we already have and neglect the One who we really need?**

I know there are those who will say, "well, God knows what we mean when we pray". Of that I have no doubt since God knows all things. The question is not whether God knows what you mean, but rather do you know what you mean? If you do not know what to ask for, or what you are entitled to as a believer, you can ask for and be believing for the wrong things. So, God may know what you mean but what you mean may not line up with His way.

The Kingdom of God works this way, *"faith comes by hearing and hearing by the Word of God"*. So if you do not know what you are entitled to, and your understanding of the anointing is wrong, you will not know how to pray and your faith will not have the substance necessary to activate the power of the miraculous in your life. Yet, when you hear the truth about the anointing, and as a result come to a greater understanding of it, your faith will rise to the call and produce amazing results for you; and not only you, but those whom the Lord has called you to minister to.

The Kingdom of God works this way, *"But you shall receive power when the Holy Spirit comes upon you"*. Are you tired of not seeing the Hand of God moving in your life and in your ministry? Do you feel powerless and ineffective in your service to God? Then understand this, it is God the Father, God the Son, and God the

Holy Spirit, period. Stop treating the anointing as if it were God the Father, God the Son, God the Holy Spirit, and the Anointing. Begin to realize that what you are looking for is not more anointing, but more of the Holy Spirit.

The anointing is the process of being marked and set apart by God, anointed for His service, and endued with power as the Holy Spirit works through the anointing on your life. Because of what Jesus accomplished on the cross, if you believe and receive His offer of salvation, you are now holy and anointed. As a result, God the Father can now use you in His service. **Just as true, He wants to use you.**

The devil's purpose is to discredit God and convince the world that He does not exist, or if He does exist, to convince them that He either does not care or is too powerless to save them. We have been called and set apart by God, **anointed** by God, to show the world that God does exist and that His ear is not too dull to hear, and His arm is not too short to save.

In this chapter we have seen that the power of the anointing is the Holy Spirit. We looked at scriptural references in both the Old and New Testaments which confirms this truth. Now let us take a look at the one and only book in the entire Bible that was written exclusively to record the acts of the New Covenant church in operation. This is of course, the Book of Acts. It is interesting to note that throughout this entire book, with all the recorded miracles contained within it, you hardly ever see the word "anointing" mentioned. In fact, the only time the anointing is mentioned in the Book of Acts is when it is referring to Jesus. Did you ever take a moment to think about that? I mean, with all the times and occasions the modern-day church refers to the anointing whenever the miraculous is in operation, does this not give us cause to stop and reflect on our use of the word anointing?

Here are the only two verses of scripture in the entire book of Acts that mention the anointing:

Acts 4:27

For of a truth against thy holy child Jesus, <u>whom thou hast</u> anointed, both Herod, and Pontius Pilate, with the Gentiles, and the people of Israel, were gathered together, ... KJV

Acts 10:38

<u>How God</u> anointed Jesus of Nazareth <u>with the Holy Ghost and with power</u>: who went about doing good, and healing all that were oppressed of the devil; for God was with him. KJV

However, in the modern-day church whenever the power of God shows up in a service or upon an individual, we are quick to declare, "the anointing". Wouldn't it make sense that with the frequency in which the modern-day church uses the word "anointing", that we would see the early church mention it at least once, maybe twice, whenever the power of God showed up on the scene?

In the Book of Acts, we see many recorded instances of the miraculous at work without the word "anointing" ever being mentioned. We can conclude that the reason the early church did not mention the anointing with the frequency that the present-day church does is that they understood what the anointing really was.

Acts 1:8 But ye shall receive power after that the Holy Ghost is come upon you: and ye shall be witnesses unto me both in Jerusalem, and in all Judaea, and in Samaria, and unto the uttermost part of the earth. KJV

> *Acts 4:33 And with great power gave the apostles witness of the resurrection of the Lord Jesus and great grace was upon them all.* KJV

Do you see the word "anointing" mentioned in either of these two verses of scripture? I do not. Let me make this clear, this does not mean that the anointing is not in operation throughout the book of Acts, on the contrary, the anointing is in operation throughout the entire book. **The early church always referred to the power of the anointing whenever the anointing was in operation.**

Let us look at a portion of scripture found in the Book of Acts where I will show you the anointing in operation. I will do this by applying this *symbol with wording I interject in parenthesis. In this scripture we will see the result of what happened after the promise of the Holy Spirit came upon the church, the Lord's anointed.

> *Acts 4:33 And with great power* *(the result of the Holy Spirit empowering the anointed) *gave the apostles witness of the resurrection of the Lord Jesus* *(the purpose of the anointing): *and great grace was upon them all.* KJV

The Book of Acts gives us a record of what happened through the Apostles *after* the Holy Spirit fell on the day of Pentecost and empowered their anointing. *Keep in mind that the Apostles were anointed the moment Jesus chose them and appointed them, but they had no power until the Holy Spirit came upon them.* Jesus left us the same example in the Gospels. He was anointed from His natural birth but did not do anything miraculous until the Holy Ghost empowered Him.

This is very important, and we must all take this to heart, these verses also make it very clear that the Holy Spirit empowering the anointing in the New Testament church is for the sole purpose of glorifying Jesus and His completed work on the cross. **The** anointing is never for showing how great we are, but always to show how great God is.

To sum it up; the Biblical concept and application of the anointing is immensely powerful. But, the power of the anointing has and always will be, the Holy Spirit. So therefore, follow the leading of the scriptures and pray for those things the Bible actually encourages us to pray for.

Luke 11:13

13 "If you then, being evil, know how to give good gifts to your children, how much more shall your heavenly Father give the Holy Spirit to those who ask Him?" NASB

As believers in Christ, you are anointed. There are no exceptions to this. Every Born Again believer has two unique anointings that God has placed upon their lives. He has placed these anointings on our lives to empower us to be the witnesses He commanded us to be. In the next chapter we will look at the two anointings each and every believer has upon their life.

CHAPTER 4

The Two Anointings of the Believer

The New Covenant Blessing

IN OUR SEARCH to understand the anointing, it is vital to realize that the New Covenant operates on a different set of rules than the Old Covenant did. This applies to the anointing as well. The anointing plays an incredibly significant role in the New Covenant church just as it did in the Old Covenant church. However, and this is particularly important, concerning the "who is anointed", and the "why they are anointed", changes dramatically in the New Covenant from the Old Covenant.

I would like to take a moment to show you how the Old Covenant hangs a shadow over the present-day church regarding the anointing. In the Old Covenant, only a few select men were anointed. But, in the New Covenant, every single Born Again Believer, both men and women, are anointed. In the Old Covenant, there were those who were anointed as either Kings or Priests. In the New Covenant, all believers are anointed as both Kings and Priests. In the book of 1st Peter, believers are called a "Royal Priesthood". In the book of

Revelation, we the believer, are referred to as Kings and Priests; not once, but three times.

1 Peter 2:*9 But ye are a chosen generation, a <u>royal priesthood,</u> an holy nation, a peculiar people; that ye should shew forth the praises of him who hath called you out of darkness into his marvellous light:* **KJV**

Rev 1:5-6

5 And from Jesus Christ, who is the faithful witness, and the first begotten of the dead, and the prince of the kings of the earth. Unto him that loved us, and washed us from our sins in his own blood,

6 And <u>hath made us kings and priests</u> unto God and his Father; to him be glory and dominion for ever and ever. Amen. KJV

Revelation 5:9 And they sung a new song, saying, Thou art worthy to take the book, and to open the seals thereof: for thou wast slain, and hast redeemed us to God by thy blood out of every kindred, and tongue, and people, and nation;10 And hast made us unto our God <u>kings and priests</u>: and we shall reign on the earth.

Revelation 20:6 Blessed and holy is he that hath part in the first resurrection: on such the second death hath no power, but they shall be <u>priests</u> of God and of Christ, and shall <u>reign</u> with him a thousand years. KJV

It may interest you to know that God's original intention was to raise up Israel to be a nation of Kings and Priests. However, because the people were not willing, only a select few were anointed during the Old Covenant dispensation.

That same mentality looms over the church today. This thinking that only a select few are anointed, while the rest must struggle in this life doing their best in their own strength has no place in the New Testament Church. This school of thought may be a good excuse for those who find themselves powerless and ineffective in their service to God, but it falls miserably short of God's instructions for how His people are to operate in this life.

One of the greatest blessings of the New Testament church is the indisputable truth that the Lord has placed His anointing upon every single believer.

The Two Anointing's Every New Testament Believer Has:

1. Kingly Anointing
2. Priestly Anointing

1) We as believers are anointed as Kings.

In the Old Covenant, men were anointed as Kings for the purpose of reigning in life, advancing the Kingdom, and exercising authority over their enemies. This is exactly what the Born-Again Believer is anointed to do in the New Covenant.

We are anointed to Reign in life.

1 Corinthians 4:8 Now ye are full, now ye are rich, ye have reigned as kings without us: and I would to God ye did reign, that we also might reign with you. KJV

Romans 5:7...; much more they which receive abundance of grace and of the gift of righteousness shall reign in life by one, Jesus Christ. KJV

We are anointed to advance the Kingdom of God.

Mark 16:15-16 - "And He said to them (the believers), 'Go into all the world and preach the gospel to all creation. He who has believed and has been baptized shall be saved; ...

We are anointed to exercise authority over all our enemies.

Mark 16:17-18 And these signs will accompany those who have believed: in My name they will cast out demons, they will speak with new tongues; they will pick up serpents, and if they drink any deadly poison, it shall not hurt them; they will lay hands on the sick, and they will recover.'" NASB

This applies to all believers. Not just the Apostle, the Prophet, the Evangelist, but all believers. Are you a believer? Then you are anointed to do all these things that Jesus declares the believer would be able to do. Did you know that there is not one account in all the Word of God where anyone failed to accomplish that which they were anointed to do? Jesus anointed you to do these signs and wonders. You are anointed to lay hands on the sick. You are anointed to cast out devils. It says so right here in the Gospel of Mark.

This is the day and the hour of the church. God is raising up a church in these last days that is not made up merely of members, but of anointed men and women who are going to wreak havoc on the devil. The Lord is raising up a church that knows what it is to walk in the power of the Holy Spirit.

The Word of God says, *"You shall know the truth, and the truth shall make you free".*

<u>**This is the truth:**</u>

Mark 16:17 And these signs shall follow them that believe; In my name shall they cast out devils; they shall speak with new tongues;

18.They shall take up serpents; and if they drink any deadly thing, it shall not hurt them; they shall lay hands on the sick, and they shall recover.

<u>**This is the freedom:**</u>

Mark 16:20 And they went forth, and preached everywhere, the Lord working with them, and confirming the word with signs following. Amen. KJV

Jesus said of Himself, *"The Spirit of the Lord is upon me, because He has anointed Me..."*, He believed it therefore He spoke. You must believe and now speak (confess) that, **"The Spirit of the Lord is upon me, because He has anointed me, and He has anointed me to do the works of Christ."**

Jesus was the first, the Bible says, of many brethren. He was the first of many anointed ones. He said, *"Truly, truly, I say to you, he who believes in Me, the works that I do shall he do also; and greater works than these shall he do; because I go to the Father." John 14:12.* NASB

In other words what Jesus was saying is this, "I am delegating the power that I have to you. The Holy Spirit that is empowering

Me, shall come and empower you." Do you believe this? I do! This is where faith comes in along with your anointing. You must believe that you are anointed, and <u>you must know what your anointing is</u>.

> *2 Corinthians 5:17 Therefore if any man be in Christ, he is a new creature: old things are passed away; behold, all things are become new.*
>
> *18 And all things are of God, who hath reconciled us to himself by Jesus Christ, and <u>hath given to us the ministry of reconciliation;</u>*
>
> *19 To wit, <u>that God was in Christ</u>, reconciling the world unto himself, not imputing their trespasses unto them; <u>and hath committed unto us</u> the word of reconciliation.*

20 <u>Now then we are ambassadors for Christ</u>, ..." KJV

This is what makes us Christians.

> **The name CHRISTIAN was first given at Antioch to Christ's followers. It is the Christians mission to spread the gospel to the world with signs and wonders following.**

Jesus declared, ***"The Spirit of the Lord is upon me, because He has anointed me to preach the gospel..."***, Lk 4:18. Now He has anointed you to go and preach the gospel. You may say, who am I? It does not matter who you are, it is what you are; and <u>you are anointed</u>.

Being a Christian is more than just being someone who believes in Christ and knows they are on their way to heaven. The true meaning of being a Christian is defined in the very life and works of Jesus Himself. Jesus came to set the standard. The Apostles knew this. When it was their turn to be filled with the Holy Spirit, they knew just what to do with His power.

Jesus spent three and a half years imparting to His disciples. He spent much of this time pouring into their lives and preparing them to take up where He left off. Meanwhile, the disciples spent that time **drawing from His anointing** so that on the day of Pentecost they were ready to kick into action.

There are many great men and women in the Kingdom of God today who walk in their anointing. Find them, seek them out, and connect with them. One of the fastest ways to kick start your anointing is for you to get in the presence of those who walk in the power of their anointing, and then **begin to draw from them**. Catch the fire that they burn in, be inspired by the energy that the anointing in their lives generates and be stirred on to greatness. Do not settle for mediocrity, but rather renounce all dry and dead expressions of Christianity as a false representation. Let us declare like Paul, **"That I might know Him and the Power of His resurrection"**. Philippians 3:10

If in the Old Testament there was not even one instance where anyone who was anointed ever failed to operate in that which they were anointed to do, how can we, the New Testament church, even for one moment, dare to entertain the thought that we could ever fail to do what we have been anointed to do?

In the Old Covenant, they would anoint the people with oil. The oil represents a type of the Holy Ghost. Jesus was not anointed with oil; **He was anointed with the Holy Spirit.** You and I are not anointed with mere oil, we are anointed with the same Holy Spirit with which Jesus was anointed. We are anointed with the real thing; it is not just a smearing of oil anymore that can be seen. You cannot see it with the natural eyes, but when someone is walking in their anointing you will know it. You know that person has that "special something" which makes them "no longer common."

If you are in a church where you are told that only the Pastors and the Apostles and the Evangelists can operate in the power of the Holy Ghost, get out of there. This is the hour of the church. The days of just one or two individuals operating in the extraordinary power of God is over. The Holy Spirit greatly desires to move through His anointed vessels. Do not be like so many saints who pray for revival and then quench the Holy Spirit when He comes to answer their prayers.

Make This Your Confession Based upon Your Kingly Anointing: "Through my Kingly Anointing I will reign in this life, I will exercise authority over all my enemies, and I will continually be active in advancing the Kingdom of God through the power of the Holy Spirit".

2) We as believers are Anointed as Priests

Malachi 2:7

7 "For the lips of a priest should preserve knowledge, and men should seek instruction from his mouth; for he is the messenger of the LORD of hosts. NASB

We began this chapter with the New Testament truth that we are partakers of a better covenant built upon better promises. So, let us understand that if we bring any Old Covenant practices into the New Covenant dispensation, we will adversely affect our anointing; a little bit of leaven, leavens the whole lump of dough. In the Old Covenant, the people of God were dependent upon the priest to mediate between God and man. In the Old Covenant, only the select few who were anointed as priests could serve in the sanctuary, offer up sacrifices, and intercede for the people. In the Old Covenant, only the select few who were anointed as priests could understand and interpret the Word of God. In the Old Covenant, only those who were anointed as priests could experience and carry the presence of the Lord. As a result, under the Old Covenant, the people of God were completely dependent upon the priests to reach God for their needs and for their wants.

In the New Covenant, every believer is anointed as priest. This may shock you, but it should not; your pastor is not your priest, he is your pastor. Your pastor is not responsible to mediate between you and God. Jesus is our Mediator, and only Jesus.

In the New Covenant our anointing as priests enables us to:

1. Serve God
2. Intercede for others
3. Experience His presence
4. Comprehend the Word of God.

The ability to comprehend the Word of God is one of the greatest blessings afforded to us as children of God. Yet so many in the church today are ignorant of this truth. There is no reason whatsoever that a believer should have any difficulty receiving revelation from the Word of God. If you struggle in trying to understand the Word of God, it is because you are unaware of your priestly anointing. As believers we have an anointing to understand, and thereby receive all the benefits that come from the Word of God.

After His resurrection, and just before ascending into heaven, Jesus imparted this anointing to all believers.

> *Luke 24:44 And he said unto them, These are the words which I spake unto you, while I was yet with you, that all things must be fulfilled, which were written in the law of Moses, and in the prophets, and in the psalms, concerning me.*
>
> *45 Then opened he their understanding, that they might understand the scriptures, 46 And said unto them, Thus it is written... KJV*

The Apostle John confirms this very same anointing:

> **1 John 2:27 - "And as for you, <u>the anointing which you received from Him abides in you</u>, and you have no need for anyone to teach you; but as <u>His anointing teaches you about all things</u> and is true and is not a lie, and just as it has taught you, you abide in Him".** NASB

Without the anointing, all you have is knowledge without life. Our priestly anointing enables us to understand spiritual truths when we read the Word of God; it also gives us ears to hear what the Spirit is saying to the church when we hear the preaching of God's word.

Let the Word of God get into your heart (spirit) by way of the anointing, and then your heart will instruct and renew your mind. **"..., but be transformed by the renewing of your mind, that you may prove what the will of God is, that which is good and acceptable and perfect."** Romans 12:2

It is **"...the Spirit (that) gives life."** 2 Corinthians 3:6. The church needs to get out of the realm of the mind and start yielding to their anointing. The church needs to draw from their anointing and let the Holy Spirit teach them the word and deliver it to their heart where it belongs. This is what will make the church free, not counseling, not coddling the flesh, but knowing the truth. You shall know the truth, and the truth shall make you free.

> **John 16:13-14 - "But when He, the Spirit of truth, comes, He will guide you into all the truth; for He will not speak on His own initiative, but whatever He hears, He will speak; and He will disclose to you what is to come. He shall glorify Me; for He shall take of Mine and shall disclose it to you."** NASB

Jesus taught us that this is the work of the Holy Spirit, guiding us into truth (the Word) and disclosing (teaching - depositing) it into us. **The Holy Spirit works through your anointing**. He will give you understanding if you will let Him. This is a very vital part of His work here on earth. Your anointing gives you every right to expect the Holy Spirit to reveal the Word of God to you. Every time I open the Bible, I ask the Holy Spirit to illuminate the word to me and help me to understand it, every single time.

The Word of God is of the Spirit. It is foolishness to the natural man, for he cannot discern the things of the Spirit. I am anointed to understand what the Word of God says. When I sit in a service and someone teaches or preaches to me, I am anointed to understand what that person says. That is why we should not get upset with people when (forgive my strong wording), they are as thick as a brick. You wonder, when are they going to get it? The reason they never get it is that they are hearing the Word with their mind and they never let it get into their spirits. They are hearing the same message, but they are not responding. They are hearing the same word you and I are hearing, but they are not changing. Why? The answer is not that I am smarter or better, or that God loves me more. It is that I have recognized the anointing God gave to me, and to all believers, and I have learned to draw from that anointing.

> *Jeremiah 23:29 "Is not My word like fire?" declares the LORD, "and like a hammer which shatters a rock?* NASB

Let the anointing turn the Word of God into fire and into a hammer that will burn away all the chaff and shatter every yoke the enemy would try to place in your life. The Word of God has the power to do this and the Holy Spirit can deliver it to you.

Before you read the Word of God, pray this first:

"Lord I thank you for anointing me with the ability to understand Your word. Holy Spirit, I ask you to grant me the wisdom to receive from your word everything that you have for me."

You will begin to see great results when you learn to draw from your priestly anointing.

We just looked at the two anointings each and every believer shares in common. But it may interest you to know that there are many other anointings which the Lord places upon certain individuals in His body, and these anointings are for a specific purpose. In the next chapter, we will look at some of these anointings.

CHAPTER 5

Anointed for a Specific Purpose

IN THIS CHAPTER we are going to see that when you are anointed, you are marked and set apart for a <u>specific</u> purpose. We will also come to understand that just because someone is anointed in one area, it does not mean that they are anointed in another. The Word of God shows us very clearly in both the Old and New Testaments that there are different anointing's delegated to different people. The Word of God also shows us that each of these unique anointings have their set purpose in the Kingdom of God.

Though every believer in the New Covenant has upon their life the anointing of King and Priest, there are also "Specific Anointings" placed upon certain individuals by the Lord. The Word of God tells us in the fourth chapter of Ephesians, that the purpose of this is for the building up of His church. It is important to note that though these anointings are given primarily to build up His Church, they also play a vital role in reaching the world for Christ.

Let us see how the Word of God clearly and undeniably points out that people are anointed for a specific purpose.

Exodus 29:1 And this is the thing that thou shalt do unto them to hallow them (Aaron and his sons),

*to minister unto me in the <u>priest's office</u>: ... 7
Then shalt thou take the anointing oil, and
pour it upon his head, and anoint him....: and
the priest's office shall be theirs for a perpetual
statute: and thou shalt consecrate Aaron and his
sons.* KJV

God instructs Moses to anoint Aaron and his sons to the office
of Priest, not King, not Prophet. Moses anointed Aaron and his sons
with oil to separate them unto the purpose and functionality of the
priesthood. It is also worthy to note that in this portion of scripture
the Word of God makes it truly clear that it is God, not man, Who
decides who gets anointed and for what purpose. When it comes
to the anointing, the Bible makes it clear that God, and only God,
does the choosing.

Let us look at some other specific anointings in the Word of God.
In this next portion of scripture, the Lord is giving Elijah instructions
on anointing three <u>different</u> people for three <u>different</u> purposes.

1 Kings 19:15-16 "And the Lord said to him
(Elijah), *'Go return on your way to the wilderness
of Damascus, and when you have arrived, you
shall <u>anoint Hazael king over Aram</u>; and Jehu the
son of Nimshi you shall <u>anoint king over Israel</u>;
and Elisha the son of Shaphat of Abel-mehola you
shall <u>anoint as prophet</u> in your place.'"* NASB

The Lord directed Elijah to anoint Hazael and Jehu as Kings,
each one over their own <u>specific area</u>, and Elisha, He wanted anointed
as a Prophet. Even though Elisha and Jehu were both anointed, it is
clear to see that Elisha did not have the same anointing as Jehu. If
Elisha, as great a Prophet as he was, would try to be King in Jehu's
place, he would have been powerless and ineffective in that role.

As anointed as Jehu was to be King over Israel, he was not

anointed to be a Prophet. If he were to try and be a Prophet in the place of Elijah, he would have been a false Prophet. Why? Because he was not anointed to be a Prophet, he was anointed to be a King. Was Jehu anointed? Yes, but not as a Prophet. **What is a False Prophet? Someone that has not been anointed to be a Prophet and yet acts as if he is one.**

This is an especially important revelation to have in the church today. We must understand that just because someone has the gift of prophecy, one of the nine gifts of the Holy Spirit operating in their life, it does not mean that they have been anointed to the office of a Prophet. **The Prophet is an anointing, prophecy is a gift of the Spirit.** There are many circles in the church today that mistakenly call people "Prophets" simply because they can prophesy. The gift of prophecy does not qualify anyone to be a Prophet, only the anointing of the Prophet qualifies someone to be a Prophet. The gift of prophecy may appear from time to time, but the office of a Prophet functions 24/7.

It is extremely important that we operate only in the anointing which the Lord has given us. If you are anointed by God to an office or a specific work of service, no one will be able to hold you back. If you are not anointed for a specific work of service, it would be best that someone would hold you back.

The Bible shows us a very sobering account of a man who was anointed as King, yet he took it upon himself to play the role of a Priest, a role for which he was not anointed:

> *2 Chronicles 26:3 Uzziah was sixteen years old* <u>*when he became king,*</u> *and he reigned fifty-two years in Jerusalem; ...4 And he did right in the sight of the LORD according to all that his father Amaziah had done. 5 And he continued to seek God in the days of Zechariah, who had*

understanding through the vision of God; and as long as he sought the LORD, God prospered him.

2 Chronicles 26:16 But when he became strong, his heart was so proud that he acted corruptly, and he was unfaithful to the LORD his God, for he entered the temple of the LORD to burn incense on the altar of incense. 17 Then Azariah the priest entered after him and with him eighty priests of the LORD, valiant men. 18 And they opposed Uzziah the king and said to him, "It is not for you, Uzziah, to burn incense to the LORD, but for the priests, the sons of Aaron who are consecrated (anointed) to burn incense. Get out of the sanctuary, for you have been unfaithful, and will have no honor from the LORD God." 19 But Uzziah, with a censer in his hand for burning incense, was enraged; and while he was enraged with the priests, the leprosy broke out on his forehead before the priests in the house of the LORD, beside the altar of incense. 20 And Azariah the chief priest and all the priests looked at him, and behold, he was leprous on his forehead; and they hurried him out of there, and he himself also hastened to get out because the LORD had smitten him. 21 And King Uzziah was a leper to the day of his death; and he lived in a separate house, being a leper, for he was cut off from the house of the LORD. NASB

Uzziah was anointed as King, but not as a Priest. He was a great King; he was a lousy Priest. That was because the anointing is specific. In the Old Testament there was an anointing for Priests,

Judges, Kings, and Prophets. We see this very clearly in the Word of God.

Let us see what the New Testament has to say about this:

Ephesians 4:11 And he (the Lord) gave some, apostles; and some, prophets; and some, evangelists; and some, pastors and teachers; KJV

The New Testament says that He, the Lord, gave **"some"**, not **"all"**. Here the Apostle Paul lists the anointings we commonly refer to as the "Five-Fold Ministry". Paul also shows us that it is the Lord who controls the distribution of the anointing. You may say, "but I am anointed", and you may very well be. But, if the Lord has not chosen you to be placed within the Five-Fold Ministry, the anointing you have will not produce the same results as one who has been chosen for that purpose.

In this portion of scripture, we see five completely different anointing's. These five specific anointings are easily distinguishable from one another. There is the prophet, which is different from the pastor, which is different from the teacher, who is different from the apostle, which is different from the evangelist.

There are pastors who are amazing preachers, and the Spirit of the Lord operates through them under the unction of preaching and exhortation in a great and powerful way. But that does not mean they are also anointed to be a prophet. They might be, but not necessarily. There are those who operate mightily under the anointing of the prophet, but that does not mean they are anointed as a teacher. They might be, but then again, maybe not.

In *1 Timothy 3:2,* the Apostle Paul declares that all those in ministry should be able to teach (didaktikos). The actual meaning here is that they simply have the ability to instruct. However, the anointing of the teacher (didaskalos), carries with it far more authority, power and revelatory abilities than just giving instruction.

Whatever you have been anointed by the Lord to be is where

you will experience your greatest success. That is because it is the anointing on your life that determines how the power of the Holy Spirit will most effectively manifest Himself through you.

If you try to function in an anointing that you do not have, then remember this: no anointing, no assistance from the Holy Spirit. Without the Holy Spirit, what could you possibly accomplish?

> *2 Corinthians 1:21 Now he which stablisheth us*
> *with you in Christ, and hath anointed us, is God;*
> *22 Who hath also sealed us and given the earnest*
> *of the Spirit in our hearts.* KJV

The Lord told me this about the anointing, He said, **"The anointing is that which defines what we are while under the power and influence of the Holy Spirit"**. The anointing takes the power of God and manifests it through individual men and women so that they may minister effectively to the needs of the people. We all serve in the Kingdom of God, and the Kingdom functions by the power of God, and the Kingdom of God operates through the anointing. The anointing on the individual will direct which way the power of God will operate through that individual. **The anointing is not a power, it is the conduit through which the power operates.**

Let me explain it to you this way, when you look at a typical kitchen you will see many different appliances, each appliance with its own purpose and ability. **For illustrative purposes only**, let us say that the different appliances each represent a different anointing, and the electricity that powers the appliances represents the Holy Spirit. Though it is the same electricity that flows to the refrigerator as flows to the microwave, the refrigerator cools things while the microwave heats things. It is the **purpose** of the appliance that defines what happens once the **power source** flows through it.

That is the way the anointing operates. It is the purpose of your anointing that defines what will happen when the power of the

Holy Spirit flows through you. Just like the appliances. The same source of power that flows through the refrigerator, runs through the microwave. Same source of power, different function when the power is turned on.

The Apostle Paul puts it this way:

1 Corinthians 12:4 Now there are varieties of gifts, but the same Spirit. 5 And there are varieties of ministries, and the same Lord. 6 And there are varieties of effects, but the same God who works all things in all persons. 7 But to each one is given <u>the manifestation of the Spirit</u> for the common good...<u>11 But one and the same Spirit works all these things, distributing to each one individually just as He wills</u>. 12 For even as the body is one and yet has many members, and all the members of the body, though they are many, are one body, so also is Christ... 14 For the body is not one member, but many. 15 If the foot should say, "Because I am not a hand, I am not a part of the body," it is not for this reason any the less a part of the body. 16 And if the ear should say, "Because I am not an eye, I am not a part of the body," it is not for this reason any the less a part of the body. 17 If the whole body were an eye, where would the hearing be? If the whole were hearing, where would the sense of smell be? 18 <u>But now God has placed the members, each one of them, in the body, just as He desired</u>. 19 And if they were all one member, where would the body be? 20 But now there are many members, but one body. NASB

The same blood that flows and gives life to the ear, flows and gives life to the eye. Yet, the eye sees, and the ear hears.

I am anointed as a teacher and as a pastor, and evangelist *(an evangelist is someone who is anointed to convert others to the Christian faith)*. Most of the time when I stand to minister, and the Holy Spirit comes upon me and **empowers me** (some would improperly say anoints me), I will find myself moving under the teaching anointing. When I stand before a congregation and teach, the Holy Spirit is not anointing me, rather He is **empowering the anointing** I already possess. The Holy Spirit empowers our anointing and that is the manifestation the people of God will experience. When I stand before the lost, at funerals, weddings, on street corners, or large events, it is not a teacher that they need, they need an evangelist. My anointing as evangelist already exists, I do not need to be anointed again, I need my anointing as evangelist to be empowered by the Holy Spirit.

> **Acts 13:1 Now there were in the church that was at Antioch certain <u>prophets</u> and <u>teachers;</u> ... 2 As they ministered to the Lord, and fasted, the <u>Holy Ghost</u> said <u>Separate</u> me <u>Barnabas and Saul for the work whereunto I have called them</u>...4 So they, being sent forth by the Holy Ghost, ...** KJV

The Lord decides who is to be raised up and set apart for ministry. He does this through His pastors and prophets. The pastor and the prophet, have as part of their anointing, the ability to discern those who are called into ministry.

There are two ways to be raised up into a ministry - the right way, and the wrong way. Only the Holy Spirit working through the anointing destroys the yokes in people's lives. If you have not been raised up and called by God, then you are just doing your own thing. If you are doing your own thing then God is not obligated to bless it, the devil is not afraid of it, and the yoke that binds people will remain in place.

> Hebrews 5:4 says, *"And no one takes the honor to himself, but receives it when he is called by God, even as Aaron was."* Notice, the Word of God says *"... even as Aaron was."* Aaron was anointed by God, because God chose him.

We are not talking about the gifts of the Spirit; all Spirit filled believers can operate in the gifts of the Spirit, and believers are encouraged to pursue these gifts. But, the anointing and the gifts of the Spirit are not the same thing. One may be anointed as pastor and yet operate in the gift of prophecy. Operating in the gift of prophecy does not make the pastor a prophet, he is a pastor who prophesies. One is a gift, the other is an anointing. One may be anointed as an intercessor, yet that same individual may operate in the word of knowledge, or the discerning of spirits. There is the anointing, and there are the gifts.

The anointing is that which defines who we are and what we are called to do, while the gifts of the Spirit assist or compliment us in that calling. Another difference between the anointing and the gifts of the Spirit is that the gifts operate only as the Spirit leads, but **the anointing is permanently in operation. The anointing does not come and go, or fall upon someone and then lift. When a person is anointed, they are anointed permanently and for life.** I am anointed when I am ministering to a body of believers, and I am anointed when I am eating a hamburger.

Remember this, it is the Holy Spirit operating through the anointing upon a person's life that destroys the yoke, not a good sermon, not a good teaching. The Apostle Paul confirms this when he said, *"And my message and my preaching were not in persuasive words of wisdom, but in Demonstration of the Spirit and of Power, that your faith should not rest on the wisdom of men, but on the power of God." 1 Cor.2:4-5. NASB*

When the Holy Spirit is flowing through a person who is anointed the people will experience the power of God, every single time. The church does not need another sermon. The church needs the power of God. Good messages do not destroy the works of the devil, the Holy Spirit does. Great teachings do not tear down strongholds, the Holy Spirit working through the anointing does. Our faith can and will rest on that which comes from an anointed vessel of God, but it can never rest on just the wisdom of men.

The New Testament anointing is not limited to just apostles, prophets, evangelists, pastors and teachers. There is a diversity of anointings, just as there is a diversity of the gifts of the Spirit. For example, there are those that have an anointing for intercession, while others may have an anointing for vision and expansion. There are those who have an anointing to reach people no one else can reach such as gang members and drug addicts, and others who have an anointing for financial prosperity to help finance the Kingdom of God. There are those who have an anointing upon their lives to write songs, while others have it to sing or play an instrument. Though the anointing may vary from one saint to another, the power of that anointing remains the same.

It may not be important for you to know all the various anointings available to the church, but it is particularly important for you to know what your anointing is. There is no better place to learn this than in your local church. The Holy Spirit has, and always will, work through the local church. There is no bypassing this. Trying to discover your anointing outside of the church is not only reckless, it is dangerous. That is because part of the pastoral anointing is the ability to recognize those in their congregation who have the call of God on their lives.

There is no better way to find out if there is a calling on your life than by getting involved in your local church and being submitted to your pastor. If you believe there is a special anointing upon your life, you must submit it to the authority of your pastor and put your trust in God. Fear not, the Lord always watches over His anointed.

> **Psalms 20:6 Now know I that the LORD saveth his anointed; he will hear him from his holy heaven with the saving strength of his right hand. 7 Some trust in chariots, and some in horses: but we will remember the name of the LORD our God. 8 They are brought down and fallen: but we (the anointed) are risen, and stand upright.** KJV

Be at peace, if there is an anointing upon your life for a specific service, the Lord will not allow it to be wasted. Being faithfully committed and consistently active in your church is the one thing all who are truly anointed by God have in common. You must realize that just attending church is not good enough. When someone is indeed anointed for a specific service, laziness is never a part of his or her lifestyle. There is just something about the Lord's anointed, they are always about the Father's business.

Now I realize that there are some of you reading this who are active in your local church, but feel inadequate and ineffective in your service. That is why it is so important for you to understand the anointing. There are many in the Body of Christ today who are anointed for the position they hold in their local church, and yet, they have not even begun to tap into the power that is available to them to fulfill their ministry. The lack of understanding the anointing is hindering many from becoming dynamos for the Kingdom of God.

This same lack of understanding is also causing many to judge wrongly and, at times, criticize those who are genuinely anointed. There is much confusion in the Body of Christ when it comes to this topic. **There are those who fast and pray for an anointing; that is unscriptural.** There are those who do the same for an increase in their anointing; **that is also unscriptural**. Please, please, go through the Word of God from Genesis to Revelation and show me just once, just once, where you see anyone praying for the anointing, or praying for an increase of the anointing.

The anointing does not increase, it defines. You do not pray for it, because it is the Lord who anoints. If we would be honest, we would admit that many of us do not know what the anointing is. If you do not know what it is, you cannot possibly know how to flow in it.

If you are anointed for a particular service of ministry, that is what you are anointed for. If you are anointed as a musician, then focus on being a musician and do not try to be an evangelist. If you are anointed as an intercessor, then focus on being an intercessor and do not try to be a pastor. The anointing is specific.

Remember, the anointing is not like the gifts of the Spirit. Though we are encouraged to pray for the gifts, nowhere in the Word of God does it instruct us to covet or pray for the anointing. I know this statement may bother some people because they have been encouraged to pray and fast for more anointing. You cannot receive more anointing. Your anointing can receive more power, but you cannot receive more anointing. You either are, or are not, anointed. **You cannot be more pastor, more evangelist, more prophet.** You either are or you are not, but you cannot be more.

If you are anointed, then the anointing you have is sufficient, because the Word of God shows us that the anointing is sufficient. Any insufficiency comes from our lack of understanding, not from a lack of the anointing. Yes, there are those who demonstrate a *more powerful* anointing than what is typical, but it is not that they have *more* anointing, it is that they have more of the Holy Spirit operating through their anointing. Remember Elijah and Elisha?

Elisha did not ask Elijah for more anointing, he asked for more of the Spirit that was working through Elijah's anointing. He asked for more of the Holy Spirit. This was because Elisha understood that you cannot be *more* anointed, but you can have a greater measure of the Holy Spirit operating through your anointing. I would encourage everyone to pray for the Holy Spirit to empower their anointing in a greater way.

I end this chapter with this thought: if we are going to use the Bible as our guidebook, then let us use the Bible as our guidebook. If it is not in the Bible, then it is not in there for a reason. If it is in the Bible, then it is in there for a reason. If what we say does not have its roots in the Bible, then it came from man. No matter how great that man may have been, it is still from man. Nowhere in the Bible will you ever find anyone praying for more anointing. Nowhere. The Bible is extremely specific when dealing with the anointing. We need to follow that pattern and deal with the anointing the same exact way it is outlined in the Bible.

It is not my intention to bring correction to anyone. Nor am I being disrespectful towards great men and women of God who have spoken in these ways about the anointing. Those who know me well know that I could never do that. If you want to continue to speak about the anointing and say such things as, "more anointing", "double portion of the anointing", or "fresh anointing"; go right ahead. We have been speaking this way for far too many years now; and I am sure many of us will continue to go on speaking this way. But the Bible is extremely specific when dealing with the anointing, and we really do need to follow the pattern set forth in the Word of God and deal with the anointing in the same exact way the Bible does.

One of the most encouraging things the Bible has to say about the anointing, and it is truly clear about this, is that the anointing is permanent. In the next chapter, we will see how the Bible goes through great lengths to show us that when one is anointed, they are anointed for life. It is not possible to lose the anointing.

CHAPTER 6

The Anointing is Permanent

THERE ARE THOSE who believe that we can lose our anointing. I do not believe that is possible; and in this chapter, I will show you how I came to that conclusion.

Far too many saints have suffered needlessly with condemnation, oppression, doubt, and even fear, believing that they have somehow lost their anointing. This is just not so.

When God anoints you, you are anointed for life. You may flow with it, or you may fight it; that is completely up to you. What is not up to you is to change it. When you are marked, anointed, and set apart by God, you are marked for life. It is actually that simple.

Remember, the power of the anointing is the Holy Spirit. But if there is unrepentant sin in your life, He may lift His presence from you, leaving you powerless and ineffective. But your anointing will remain. If the Holy Spirit should lift His presence from you for whatever reason, whether it is because of disobedience, continued sin, or stubbornly trying to function in another's anointing, if you will repent, He will return because you are anointed.

One would be hard pressed to find any place in the Bible where it mentions someone losing their anointing. You would think that if it were possible for a person to lose their anointing, that it would be mentioned at least once in the Bible. But it is not. It is true that you will find more than enough accounts of anointed people falling into sin and some even perishing for it. But you will never find anywhere in the Bible where they lost their anointing. You may find that hard to believe, but it is true.

> *Numbers 23:19 God is not a man, that he should lie, nor a son of man, that he should change his mind.* NIV

Since God is the One Who chooses who to call and who to place His anointing upon, the only way someone could lose their anointing would be for God to change His mind. Yet, the Bible clearly states He does not do that. He knows the beginning and the end. He alone is the author and finisher of our faith. He does not make mistakes. He knows exactly who to call and what to call them for. What they do with that calling is another story.

> *Romans 11:29 for the gifts and the calling of God are irrevocable.* NASB

Again, let me say this, though the anointing is permanent, the Holy Spirit can lift His presence off someone's life if they go astray. I would be far more concerned about grieving the Holy Spirit than losing my ministry. Do you understand this? David obviously did. Let us listen to the words of David, the one who God referred to as a man after His own heart.

> *Psalm 51:4-11*
> *4 Against Thee, Thee only, I have sinned,*
> *And done what is evil in Thy sight, ...*
> *11 Do not cast me away from Thy presence,*
> <u>*And do not take Thy Holy Spirit from me.*</u> NASB

It certainly looks to me that David was more concerned about losing the Holy Spirit than his anointing as King. It would do the church much good if more people would feel the same way and be more concerned about the possibility of offending the Holy Spirit than losing their title.

David's prayer that he would not lose the presence of the Holy Spirit in his life had much to do with what he saw happen to King Saul. As a man of God, I find the portions of scripture relating to King Saul to be the most sobering in all of scripture.

> *1 Samuel 10:1 Then Samuel took a flask of oil and poured it on Saul's head and kissed him, saying, "Has not the LORD anointed you leader over his inheritance?* NIV

After being anointed, Saul disobeyed God and as a result the Lord rejected him from being King. It is interesting to note that even though Saul was rejected as King, his anointing remained on him. You would think if one could lose their anointing this would be the place in the Bible where God would make an example of this. But instead, He uses this as an opportunity to show us that the anointing is permanent.

> *1 Samuel 16:1 And the LORD said unto Samuel, How long wilt thou mourn for Saul, seeing I have rejected him from reigning over Israel? fill thine horn with oil, and go, I will send thee to Jesse the Bethlehemite: for I have provided me a king among his sons.* KJV

As the sons of Jesse passed in front of Samuel one by one, it was not until David appeared that the Lord said to the prophet, *Arise, anoint him: for this is he.*

> *1 Samuel 16:13 Then Samuel took the horn of oil,*
> *and anointed him in the midst of his brethren:*
> *<u>and the Spirit of the LORD came upon David</u>*
> *<u>from that day forward</u>. So Samuel rose up, and*
> *went to Ramah. 14 <u>But the Spirit of the LORD</u>*
> *<u>departed from Saul</u>, and an evil spirit from the*
> *LORD troubled him.* KJV

It is clearly recorded in scripture that it was the Spirit of the Lord, the Holy Spirit, that left Saul, not the anointing. This is confirmed by a statement which David makes regarding King Saul many years later. King Saul had strayed so far from the Lord that he spent much of his time pursuing David in order to kill him. He did this in an effort to prevent David from becoming King in his place.

> *1 Samuel 24:2 Then Saul took three thousand*
> *chosen men out of all Israel, and went to seek*
> *David and his men upon the rocks of the wild*
> *goats. 3 And he came to the sheepcotes by the way,*
> *where was a cave; and Saul went in to cover his*
> *feet: and David and his men remained in the*
> *sides of the cave. 4 And the men of David said*
> *unto him, Behold the day of which the LORD said*
> *unto thee, Behold, I will deliver thine enemy into*
> *thine hand, that thou mayest do to him as it shall*
> *seem good unto thee. Then David arose, and cut*
> *off the skirt of Saul's robe privily. 5 And it came*
> *to pass afterward, that David's heart smote him,*
> *because he had cut off Saul's skirt. 6 And he said*
> *unto his men, The LORD forbid that I should do*
> *this thing unto my master, <u>the LORD's anointed</u>,*
> *to stretch forth mine hand against him, seeing <u>he</u>*
> *<u>is the anointed of the LORD</u>.* KJV

Though God had clearly rejected Saul as King, and even though the Spirit of the Lord had departed from him, the Bible takes great care to declare to us that Saul was still anointed. If one could lose their anointing, don't you think this would be a good opportunity to bring this out for us all to see? Instead, the Bible makes it truly clear that it was not the anointing which King Saul had lost, it was the Spirit of the Lord; the anointing remained, but the power left.

Sad to say, there is no record of King Saul ever repenting. Not so in the account of Samson, he did repent. There is no greater example in all the Word of God on the permanence of the anointing than that of the Old Testament judge, Samson.

> *Judges 13:1 And the children of Israel did evil again in the sight of the LORD; and the LORD delivered them into the hand of the Philistines forty years. 2 And there was a certain man of Zorah, of the family of the Danites, whose name was Manoah; and his wife was barren, and bare not. 3 And the angel of the LORD appeared unto the woman, and said unto her, Behold now, thou art barren, and bearest not: but thou shalt conceive, and bear a son. 4 Now therefore beware, I pray thee, and drink not wine nor strong drink, and eat not any unclean thing: 5 For, lo, thou shalt conceive, and bear a son; and no razor shall come on his head: for the child shall be a Nazarite unto God from the womb: and he shall begin to deliver Israel out of the hand of the Philistines.* KJV

Note: The Lord called Samson a Nazarite from the womb. The term *Nazarite* means to be separated unto God. In this case the Lord not only separated Samson unto Himself as a Nazarite, but did so for a purpose. This is exactly what the anointing is, separated unto God for a purpose.

In this next portion of scripture, I want you to notice how the Word of God takes great care to show us that it was not Samson or his anointing that performed these mighty acts of strength, but the Holy Spirit.

> *Judges 14:5 Then Samson went down to Timnah with his father and mother, and came as far as the vineyards of Timnah; and behold, a young lion came roaring toward him. 6 <u>And the Spirit of the LORD came upon him mightily</u>, so that he tore him as one tears a kid though he had nothing in his hand;...* NASB

Let us look at another account of the mighty strength which Samson displayed:

> *Judges 14:19 <u>Then the Spirit of the LORD came upon him</u> (Samson) <u>mightily</u>, and he went down to Ashkelon and killed thirty of them and took their spoil, and gave the changes of clothes to those who told the riddle.* NASB

Do you think it was the anointing that gave Samson his great power? Is it really the anointing you are feeling when God uses you mightily? Or, could it be the Spirit of God? Does the Bible say that the anointing came on Samson in a powerful way? It does not. Though Samson was anointed, it was not the anointing that gave him his power.

Let us look at one of the most famous of Samson's exploits. We will pick it up after the Philistines came down to the men of Judah and terrified them into giving Samson into their hands. From this account let us see if it was the anointing or the Holy Spirit that gave Samson his great power.

> *Judges 15:12 And they* (the men of Judah) *said to him* (Samson), *"We have come down to bind you so that we may give you into the hands of the Philistines." And Samson said to them, "Swear to me that you will not kill me." 13 So they said to him, "No, but we will bind you fast and give you into their hands; yet surely we will not kill you." Then they bound him with two new ropes and brought him up from the rock. 14 When he came to Lehi, the Philistines shouted as they met him. <u>And the Spirit of the LORD came upon him mightily</u> so that the ropes that were on his arms were as flax that is burned with fire, and his bonds dropped from his hands. 15 And he found a fresh jawbone of a donkey, so he reached out and took it and killed a thousand men with it.* NASB

I did not see the credit being given to the anointing, but I did see the Bible give the glory to the Spirit of the Lord. Many times, ill-informed Christians believe it is the anointing that performs the great works of God. Samson was anointed, yes, but it was the Holy Spirt Who gave him his great power. You may be anointed too, but it is not the anointing that gives you your power. You need to understand that if you feel you have become less effective in your service to God, it is not the anointing that has lifted from you.

Why is this so important? It is important because it is totally unreasonable for you to expect the anointing to perform that which only the Holy Spirit can do. You may very well say, "we are sealed with the Holy Spirit until the day of redemption." If you are a believer, yes that is true. But there are far too many believers who may find their way into heaven, yet have lost their way here on earth.

You have been anointed for a purpose and you will never fulfill that purpose without the Holy Spirit empowering you to accomplish it. **Serving God without the assistance of the Holy Spirit is just another form of empty powerless religion.**

If you need to purchase sermons for your Sunday morning service, or your youth group, you have lost the power of your anointing. If the only place you have victory is in church, you have lost the power of your anointing. Church is your filling station, it has been designed by God to build us up and equip us to minister to a lost and dying world, a world that so desperately needs to see the gospel demonstrated.

Here is another account from the Word of God regarding the permanence of the anointing, it should serve as a warning to all believers. Samson carelessly informs Delilah that his great strength was directly connected to a covenant made with God, and this covenant was dependent upon him never cutting his hair.

> *Judges 16:19 And she made him sleep on her knees, and called for a man and had him shave off the seven locks of his hair. Then she began to afflict him, <u>and his strength left him</u>. 20 And she said, "The Philistines are upon you, Samson!" And he awoke from his sleep and said, "I will go out as at other times and shake myself free." <u>But he did not know that the LORD had departed from him</u>. 21 Then the Philistines seized him and gouged out his eyes; and they brought him down to Gaza and bound him with bronze chains, and he was a grinder in the prison.* NASB

Please do not make the mistake of thinking Samson was the only anointed person to lose their strength and not know it. **There are** too many churches operating today which once had powerful visitations of the Holy Spirit and are now just going through the motions. Just like Samson, they do not realize that the Spirit has departed. The Apostle Paul declares that in the last days there will be those who have a form of godliness, yet they deny the power thereof.

However, as the Bible records it, Samson's hair began to grow back while he was held captive by his enemies. Thus, his covenant was restored, and the Holy Spirit returned to empower his anointing yet again.

Judges 16:22 However, the hair of his head began to grow again after it was shaved off. NASB

Judges 16:25 It so happened when they (the Philistines*) were in high spirits, that they said, "Call for Samson, that he may amuse us." So they called for Samson from the prison, and he entertained them. And they made him stand between the pillars. 26 Then Samson said to the boy who was holding his hand, "Let me feel the pillars on which the house rests, that I may lean against them."... 28* <u>*Then Samson called to the LORD and said, "O Lord GOD, please remember me and please strengthen me*</u> *just this time, O God, that I may at once be avenged of the Philistines for my two eyes." 29 And Samson grasped the two middle pillars on which the house rested, and braced himself against them, the one with his right hand and the other with his left. 30 And Samson said, "Let me die with the Philistines!" And he bent with all his might so that the house fell on the lords and all the people who were in it. So the dead whom he killed at* *his death were more than those whom he killed in his life.* NASB

When God anoints you, you are anointed forever.

Rom 11:29

29 For the gifts and calling of God are without repentance. KJV

Why is this so important for the church to understand? I will give you two reasons.

1. Your anointing was given to you by God. He chose you. He placed within you unique abilities, all of which dwell within your anointing. If you lose your way, and for whatever reason begin to serve God from outside your anointing, you will find yourself in the worst place of religion; that is, you will be serving God, who is Spirit, from the realm of the flesh. No matter how nice it may appear on the outside the flesh is always at enmity with the Spirit. If you find yourself at this place, it would be easy to think that it is the anointing which you have lost. If one were deceived into thinking this, what possible remedy could they find to replace the anointing, or possibly ever get it back? Since such a solution does not exist anywhere in the Bible, every pursuit to remedy the situation would be purely carnal and a complete waste of time. Discouragement and despair are the only possible outcomes.

2. One can only lose something they, at one time, possessed. Someone who did not actually have something could never know the feeling of loss. However, on the other hand, someone who had possessed something and then lost it, would absolutely feel the loss. It could manifest itself in

many different ways, but it is a feeling of loss just the same. There are those who are reading this who know that something has gone missing from their walk with Christ. That special energy and power that you once walked in has gone somewhere. You know you lost it, but you just do not know what it is you have lost. I can tell you with absolute certainty it is not the anointing you are looking for. One never has to look for the anointing because when someone is anointed the anointing never leaves them.

Let this be your prayer:

Psalm 51:10 Create in me a clean heart, O God,
And renew a steadfast spirit within me.
11 Do not cast me away from Thy presence,
<u>And do not take Thy Holy Spirit from me</u>.
12 Restore to me the joy of Thy salvation,
And sustain me with a willing spirit. NASB

Nowhere in the Word of God is it recorded that we are to pray, or fast, for the anointing. Nowhere. But it is His will for you to seek the One Who empowers your anointing. This is our assurance, when we pray according to His will, He hears us. If He hears us, we will have the answer to our request. This is the Word of God. It is not my opinion; it is God's revealed will. Though God is not obligated to answer prayers outside His will, He is when they are in accordance with His will.

This can be the result of praying in accordance to His will regarding the anointing:

Psalm 92:10 But Thou hast exalted my horn like that of the wild ox; <u>I have been</u> anointed with <u>fresh oil</u>. NASB

Fresh oil, not a fresh anointing. This is the scripture no doubt where many in the church mistakenly believe that there is such a thing as a fresh anointing. Just as in the case of the doctrine on a double portion of the anointing, believing in a fresh anointing is the result of misquoting the scriptures. Oil represents the Holy Spirit. It is a fresh infilling of the Holy Spirit that this scripture is referring to not a fresh anointing. There is no such thing as a fresh anointing, and whenever it is referred to in that way it is wrong, having no Biblical basis to rest upon.

There are many reasons that people feel powerless and ineffective in their anointing; and it can be traced to anything from unrepentant sin, to disobedience, and, even at times, from stubbornly trying to operate in someone else's anointing.

But I believe the most common reason people are not experiencing the power in their anointing is that they do not understand the power of **"Drawing from the Anointing"**. We will discuss this in the next chapter.

CHAPTER 7

Drawing from the Anointing

The Divine Strategy of Tapping into the Anointing for Power, Healing, and Impartation

I HAVE SHOWN you in great detail that the anointing is the conduit by which the Holy Spirit releases His power to and through the church. That said, I would like to use this chapter to show you the most effective method of tapping into this power. I believe there is simply no greater way to do this than through the process I refer to as, "Drawing from the Anointing".

If one were to ask, "what is the best way to receive from the anointing"? The answer would simply be to draw from it. Like a bucket drawing water from a well; just connect to the source and draw it out. Trust me, it is really that simple; **just connect, and draw it out**.

When you draw from the power that flows from an anointed vessel, you will receive from that power be it healing, deliverance, impartation, financial breakthrough, whatever. Once you connect by faith to the anointing on someone's life, all you need to do is draw from it; that is how you will receive your miracle or impartation.

In the gospels there are many examples of people drawing from the anointing and getting their miracles. I would like to share with you a few excellent examples that clearly show you what it means to draw from the anointing.

The woman with an issue of blood:

Luke 8:43 And a woman who had a hemorrhage for twelve years, and could not be healed by anyone, 44 came up behind Him, and touched the fringe of His cloak; and immediately her hemorrhage stopped. 45 And Jesus said, "Who is the one who touched Me?" And while they were all denying it, Peter said, "Master, the multitudes are crowding and pressing upon You." 46 But Jesus said, "Someone did touch Me, for I was aware that power had gone out of Me." 47 And when the woman saw that she had not escaped notice, she came trembling and fell down before Him, and declared in the presence of all the people the reason why she had touched Him, and how she had been immediately healed. 48 And He said to her, "Daughter, your faith has made you well; go in peace." NASB

Do you find it interesting that though there were multitudes touching Jesus and pressing against Him, not one of them received a miracle but this woman? Jesus was certainly anointed and filled with the power of the Holy Ghost, but it remained within Him. It took a woman who knew how to draw from the anointing to get that power released from Him and into her. Imagine, multitudes touching Jesus, but only one tapped into His anointing and received her miracle.

Blind Bartimaeus:

Mark 10:46 And they came to Jericho: and as he went out of Jericho with his disciples and a great number of people, blind Bartimaeus, the son of Timaeus, sat by the highway side begging. 47 And when he heard that it was Jesus of Nazareth, he began to cry out, and say, Jesus, thou Son of David, have mercy on me. 48 And many charged him that he should hold his peace: but he cried the more a great deal, <u>Thou Son of David</u>, have mercy on me.

49 And Jesus stood still, and commanded him to be called. And they call the blind man, saying unto him, Be of good comfort, rise; he calleth thee. 50 And he, casting away his garment, rose, and came to Jesus. 51 And Jesus answered and said unto him, What wilt thou that I should do unto thee? The blind man said unto him, Lord, that I might receive my sight.

52 And Jesus said unto him, Go thy way; thy faith hath made thee whole. And immediately he received his sight, ... KJV

There are three things I would like you to see from the account of Bartimaeus and how he drew from the Anointing:

1. There were multitudes all around Jesus just like the woman with the issue of blood. Yet, it is not recorded where anyone of these other people received anything from Jesus.
2. Bartimaeus connected with the anointing on Jesus. It is recorded that Bartimaeus got the Lord to stand still and give

His complete attention to him. In other words, the anointing targeted right in on Bartimaeus. When you connect with the anointing on someone's life the power flowing out from that anointing will be directed to you.

3. Bartimaeus, after connecting with the anointing, now drew from that anointing by letting the Lord know exactly what it was that he was <u>expecting</u> from Him. When it comes to drawing from the anointing **you will only receive that which you are expecting to receive!**

Both Bartimaeus and the woman with the issue of blood connected with the anointing because they were desperate. **Disinterested, and unengaged people rarely, if ever, receive anything from God.**

But there is another reason these two people received from the anointing on Jesus' life; they both knew the Word of God. This is what connected them to the anointing. Bartimaeus, and the woman with the issue of blood, knew Who Jesus was. You cannot draw from the anointing on someone's life if you do not know what their anointing is.

Son of David is the Messianic name for the coming Messiah. Bartimaeus called Jesus by this name. This got the attention of Jesus which, in turn, got Bartimaeus his miracle.

Regarding the woman with the issue of blood, she remembered what the prophet Malachi declared regarding the coming Messiah. Malachi prophesied that when the Messiah appears, whom he refers to as the, **Sun of Righteousness**, He will have healing flowing from the hem of His garment.

> **Malachi 4:2 But unto you that fear my name shall the Sun of righteousness arise with <u>healing in his wings</u>...**" KJV

Wings was a Hebrew term for what we know as the hem, or the tassels, which flow from the bottom of a garment. It is recorded that the woman with the issue of blood thought, *"If I can only touch the hem of His garment, I will be healed."* This woman recognized Who Jesus was, and she believed what His anointing could accomplish for her because she obviously knew the Word of God.

Who is your Pastor? Who are your close friends in Christ? Who are the guest ministers that stand in the pulpit of your church? You may know them by their name, but do you know them by their anointing? There are so many varieties of anointings God's people carry it would be difficult to list them all; but when you recognize and connect with the anointing on the people who God has placed in your life, you will be the better for it.

Here is another great example of what I have been saying about the importance of knowing the anointing on someone's life. In this account, Jesus was on His way to Cana of Galilee and had to pass through Samaria where He has an interesting exchange with a woman at Jacob's well.

John 4:5-14

5 So He came to a city of Samaria, called Sychar, near the parcel of ground that Jacob gave to his son Joseph; 6 and Jacob's well was there. Jesus therefore, being wearied from His journey, was sitting thus by the well. It was about the sixth hour. 7 There came a woman of Samaria to draw water. Jesus said to her, "Give Me a drink."... 9 The Samaritan woman therefore said to Him, "How is it that You, being a Jew, ask me for a drink since I am a Samaritan woman?"... 10 Jesus answered and said to her, "If you knew the gift of God, and who it is who says to you,

> *'Give Me a drink,' you would have asked Him,*
> *and He would have given you living water." 11*
> *She said to Him, "Sir, You have nothing to draw*
> *with and the well is deep; where then do You get*
> *that living water?...13 Jesus answered and said*
> *to her, "Everyone who drinks of this water shall*
> *thirst again; 14 but whoever drinks of the water*
> *that I shall give him shall never thirst; but the*
> *water that I shall give him shall become in him a*
> *well of water springing up to eternal life." NASB*

Imagine being in the very presence of the Lord, and not even knowing it. Jesus said to the woman at the well, *"If you knew the gift of God, and who it is who says to you, 'Give Me a drink,' you would have asked Him, and He would have given you living water."* I love this story, because in this account there are actually two wells one could draw from. The first was a natural well, Jacob's, where one could draw water for sustaining life. The other a supernatural well, Jesus, where one could draw living water and receive eternal life. This woman had no idea of the anointing that Jesus carried, she was only concerned with drawing from the natural water when she could have been drawing from the living water. You can only draw from the anointing on someone's life when you know what the anointing is on that person's life.

How many people do you know that whenever you leave their presence you feel refreshed and encouraged? The anointing on people's lives can do this. Some people, when you are in their company, you feel like you can run over a troop and leap over a wall. That is because the anointing is contagious, it was designed that way. Look at the Book of Judges, these anointed men, and women of God motivated others to do the impossible. It was not that the judges were great, as a matter of fact the Bible takes great care to show us that they all had weaknesses. It was because the judges were operating in their anointing. The anointing when it is in operation will always take you out of your weaknesses and catapult you into supernatural strength.

Dry ministers produce dry Christians. Ministers who know how to tap into their anointing produce motivated, fire filled Christians. If we are going to turn the world upside down like the early church did, we need to get ourselves under men and women of God who flow in their anointing. We need to get drenched in the anointing and delivered from, "dry cracker syndrome".

Apostle Tom McGuinness, my Senior Pastor for 34 years, carried a powerful anointing of breakthrough and authority. Even if my eyes were closed, I knew when he came on the altar; I would just feel a rush of strength come over me. At times when I was going through a spiritual battle it would break the very moment he stepped on the altar. This is just one of many things that can happen through anointed people with whom you connect. But you must learn how to make the connection. Many times, Apostle Tom McGuinness would stop in the middle of preaching and turn to me and say, "Pastor Anthony, I can feel you pulling on the anointing". He would say this because that was exactly what I was doing. I was pulling, I was drawing, from his anointing. I will benefit from that for the rest of my life.

The key to this is understanding that the level at which you receive from an anointed vessel is directly connected to the level of honor you sow towards that vessel.

Galatians 6:6 And let the one who is taught the word share all good things with him who teaches. 7 Do not be deceived, God is not mocked; for whatever a man sows, this he will also reap. NASB

This scripture is about far more than just money. Do not be deceived. You must sow honor to the anointed to receive from the anointing. Too many ministers have hindered the flow of their anointing because they have become critical of other anointed vessels.

Just like Samson, they do not know that the Spirit of the Lord has lifted from their anointing and they are now just ministering from experience. Too many saints have stopped receiving from the anointing because they have become fault finders and yielded to critical spirits. This can happen to anyone. Do not let it!

Listen to these warnings regarding the treatment of the Lords anointed:

> *1 Chronicles 16:22 ..., Touch not mine anointed, and do my prophets no harm.* KJV

> *Psalm 105:15 Saying, Touch not mine anointed, and do my prophets no harm.* KJV

> *Ephesians 4:29 Let no corrupt communication proceed out of your mouth, but that which is good to the use of edifying, that it may minister grace unto the hearers. 30 And grieve not the holy Spirit of God, whereby ye are sealed unto the day of redemption. 31 Let all bitterness, and wrath, and anger, and clamour, and evil speaking, be put away from you, with all malice:* KJV

According to the Apostle Paul, one sure way to grieve the Holy Spirit is to allow corrupt and evil communication to flow from your mouth toward others. If this is true, and it is, how much more when we do it against an anointed vessel? You may say, but I am anointed. That may be true, but remember, though you may be sealed until the day of redemption, having the Holy Spirit operate through your anointing is a privilege. How long do you think He will allow you this privilege if you continue to grieve Him?

I would like to share with you a confession of grace the Lord gave me. It has changed my life. I quote it on a regular basis. If you would confess this and let it get into your spirit, you will be the better for it.

"Lord, I am not better than my brothers and sisters,
I am not a fault finder,
I will not have a critical spirit,
I will not judge my brothers and sisters in Christ,
I will speak always by grace, as if seasoned with
salt."

Today, more than ever before, we need to know how to draw from the anointing, and we need to recognize what clogs up the flow. If we are going to be a witness to the world and an encouragement to the Body of Christ, we need to be vessels that know how to draw from the anointing.

Ephesians 4:11 And He gave some as <u>apostles,</u> and some as <u>prophets,</u> and some as <u>evangelists,</u> and some as <u>pastors</u> and <u>teachers,</u> 12 <u>for the equipping of the saints for the work of service, to the building up of the body of Christ;</u> NASB

Your Pastor is more than just a person with a title. Your Pastor is a person with an anointing that can build you up into a mature and stable Christian. You only need to humble yourself, submit to their authority, and learn to connect with their anointing. Next time you are in service set your eyes and ears intently on your Pastor as they are ministering, do not allow your mind to wander, give them the attention and respect they deserve. You cannot receive from someone you do not give honor to. **You must learn the beneficial practice of giving honor to, and receiving from, those anointed vessels God has placed in your life.**

Luke 10:38-42

38 Now as they were traveling along, He (Jesus) entered a certain village; and a woman named

Martha welcomed Him into her home. 39 And she had a sister called Mary, who moreover was listening to the Lord's word, seated at His feet. 40 But Martha was distracted with all her preparations; and she came up to Him, and said, "Lord, do You not care that my sister has left me to do all the serving alone? Then tell her to help me." 41 But the Lord answered and said to her, "Martha, Martha, you are worried and bothered about so many things; 42 but only a few things are necessary, really only one, for Mary has chosen the good part, which shall not be taken away from her." NASB

This story is a great example of the modern-day church. So many are so busy scurrying about doing this and doing that. Like Martha, who was so busy doing "the right thing", she neglected the "vital" thing. So many are so busy running here and there all they manage to achieve is to frustrate themselves and everyone around them. Mary chose *"the good part"*, she sat down and drew from the anointing on Jesus' life. What Mary received could *"not be taken away from her"*. Just as important, Mary now had something of value she could give to others, because she took the time to draw from the anointing.

This account was about Jesus, and it was Jesus Who was doing the teaching. And since this was Jesus teaching, His teaching was anointed. I do not see any signs and wonders operating here. I do not see the sick being healed or devils being cast out as He taught the disciples in Martha's house. But I do see the anointing in operation. When an anointed vessel is operating in their anointing do not assume that the results have to always be visible to the natural senses. Everyone who sat at Jesus' feet in Martha's house received a supernatural impartation from the Lord. Jesus, said so Himself,

"…, for Mary has chosen the good part, which shall not be taken away from her."

There is too much unbelief and misconception in the church regarding the power of anointed vessels. If I am sitting under the ministry of an anointed vessel, I am receiving from the Holy Spirit operating through the anointing upon that vessel. Every single time.

We Need to Learn How to Draw from the Anointing on Our Own Lives Too

As believers we are all anointed. We need to learn how to draw from the anointing on our own lives too. What good is your anointing if you do not live in such a way as to depend on it for everything that you do. Whether it be witnessing to the lost or serving in your local church. Even in seeking the Lord in prayer, or reading the Word of God, our anointing will help us in every area of our life.

Before I read my Bible, I call upon the Holy Spirt to empower my anointing to understand the Word of God. I have come to such a place of faith in this that not a day goes by where I do not receive fresh manna from the Word of God. I have learned how to let the Holy Spirit teach me the Word of God by tapping into my priestly anointing.

> *1 John 2:27 But the anointing which ye have received of him abideth in you, and ye need not that any man teach you: but as the same anointing teacheth you of all things, and is truth, and is no lie, and even as it hath taught you, ye shall abide in him.* KJV

Whenever I stand to minister before God's people, I first make the conscious effort to invite the Holy Spirit to empower the anointing on my life. I do this so that I will minister effectively and powerfully to His people. **I do not ask Him to anoint me, I am**

already anointed. I invite Him to empower what I know I already have. I do not waste His time or mine by praying unscriptural prayers regarding the anointing. There is no more time to waste saying prayers that only sound good and yet offer no benefit.

Learn to draw from the anointing in your life. Make it a conscious practice to invite the Holy Spirit to work through your anointing, each and every day. It is the Holy Spirit, not your anointing, Who gives you your power. The anointing only directs the way the power will manifest. Remember, as a believer you are anointed as priest and king. In this world you go out as sheep, in the midst of wolves. But if you learn the secret of drawing from the anointing the wolves will flee from your presence every single time.

There is a great account recorded in the Book of Acts of the early church <u>drawing from their anointing and waiting on the Holy Spirit to empower the anointing upon their lives</u>. Having been faced with great opposition, the church gathered together in agreement and prayed.

> *Acts 4:23-31*
>
> *23 And when they had been released, they went to their own companions, and reported all that the chief priests and the elders had said to them. 24 And when they heard this, they lifted their voices to God with one accord and said, "O Lord, it is Thou who didst make the heaven and the earth and the sea, and all that is in them, 25 who by the Holy Spirit, through the mouth of our father David Thy servant, didst say,*
>
> *'Why did the Gentiles rage,*
> *And the peoples devise futile things?*
> *26'The kings of the earth took their stand,*
> *And the rulers were gathered together*

Against the Lord, and against His Christ.'

27 "For truly in this city there were gathered together against Thy holy servant Jesus, whom Thou didst anoint, both Herod and Pontius Pilate, along with the Gentiles and the peoples of Israel, 28 to do whatever Thy hand and Thy purpose predestined to occur. 29 "And now, Lord, take note of their threats, <u>and grant that Thy bond-servants may speak Thy word with all confidence, 30 while Thou dost extend Thy hand to heal, and signs and wonders take place through the name of Thy holy servant Jesus." 31</u> And when they had prayed, the place where they had gathered together was shaken, <u>and they were all filled with the Holy Spirit,</u> and <u>began to speak the word of God with boldness.</u> NASB

Believers operating in their anointing stir up the anointed who are in their presence. There are those among us who hold the position of pastor, teacher, prophet, apostle and evangelist. Learn the secret of drawing from their anointing whenever you are in their presence. Whether my pastor was behind the pulpit, or next to me eating dinner, he was my pastor. Many times, I received as much from him outside of the pulpit as I did when he was behind the pulpit. I always honored his anointing, and I loved him faithfully up until the very moment the Lord called him home to his reward. Several months after my pastor was taken home to be with the Lord, a prophet called me out and declared over me that a great portion of the mantle that was upon my pastor now resides upon me. Why? Because I practiced the power of drawing from the anointing.

In conclusion, to really help you get this, I would like to end this book with a powerful revelation regarding the anointing on the New Testament church that few even realize exists.

After being filled with the Holy Spirit, Jesus goes into the synagogue as was His custom, and the book of Isaiah is handed to Him. He opens to the portion of scripture we know as Isaiah 61:1

> *Luke 4:16 And He came to Nazareth, where He had been brought up; and as was His custom, He entered the synagogue on the Sabbath, and stood up to read. 17 And the book of the prophet Isaiah was handed to Him. And He opened the book, and found the place where it was written, 18 "The Spirit of the Lord is upon Me, Because He anointed Me to preach the gospel to the poor.*
> *He has sent Me to proclaim release to the captives, And recovery of sight to the blind, To set free those who are downtrodden, 19 To proclaim the favorable year of the Lord."* NASB

Then it is recorded:

> *Luke 4:20 And He closed the book, and gave it back to the attendant, and sat down; and the eyes of all in the synagogue were fixed upon Him. 21 And He began to say to them, "Today this Scripture has been fulfilled in your hearing."* NASB

What I would like you to see is that Jesus read only from the portion of Isaiah 61 that pertained to Him and His earthly ministry. He stopped short of the portion of that same prophesy which was directed to His church. That is because that portion was reserved for you and me.

Let us now read this prophesy in its entirety where it first speaks of the anointing on Jesus' life and then speaks about the anointing on our lives.

Isaiah 61:1The Spirit of the Lord GOD is upon me,
Because the LORD has anointed me
To bring good news to the afflicted;
He has sent me to bind up the brokenhearted,
To proclaim liberty to captives,
And freedom to prisoners;
2 To proclaim the favorable year of the LORD,

In Jesus' earthly ministry, He fulfilled everything that He was anointed to do. Now it is up to us as His church to operate in our anointing and take up where He left off. This portion of Isaiah's prophecy applies to the New Testament Church.

And the day of vengeance of our God;
To comfort all who mourn,
3 To grant those who mourn in Zion,
Giving them a garland instead of ashes,
The oil of gladness instead of mourning,
The mantle of praise instead of a spirit of fainting.
So they will be called oaks of righteousness,
The planting of the LORD, that He may be glorified...
6 But you will be called the priests of the LORD;
You will be spoken of as ministers of our God.
You will eat the wealth of nations,
And in their riches you will boast.
7 Instead of your shame you will have a double portion,
And instead of humiliation they will shout for joy over their portion.

> *Therefore they will possess a double portion in their land,*
> *Everlasting joy will be theirs.* NASB

After prophesying about the ministry of the coming Messiah, Isaiah, goes on to prophesy about you and me. This prophesy begins with Jesus and ends with us. Because we are… **_priests of the LORD_**, and **_ministers of our God_**. Therefore, what is said about Jesus in the book of Acts, is just as true about us.

> *Acts 10:38 "You know of Jesus of Nazareth, how God anointed Him with the Holy Spirit and with power, and how He went about doing good, and healing all who were oppressed by the devil…* NASB

As a believer, God has anointed you with the Holy Ghost and power. Because of your anointing, you also have the power to go **about doing good, and healing all who are oppressed by the devil; …**

Jesus confirms this when He shares the account of why it is to our advantage that He returns to the Father and the Holy Spirit comes to take His place here with us on earth.

> *John 16:7 However, I am telling you nothing but the truth when I say it is profitable (good, expedient, advantageous) for you that I go away. Because if I do not go away, the Comforter (Counselor, Helper, Advocate, Intercessor, Strengthener, Standby) will not come to you [into close fellowship with you]; but if I go away, I will send Him to you [to be in close fellowship with you].*

John 16:13 But when He, the Spirit of Truth (the Truth-giving Spirit) comes,... 14 He will honor and glorify Me, because He will take of (receive, draw upon) what is Mine and will reveal (declare, disclose, transmit) it to you. 15 Everything that the Father has is Mine. That is what I meant when I said that He [the Spirit] will take the things that are Mine and will reveal (declare, disclose, transmit) it to you. AMP

Through the conduit of the anointing, the Holy Spirit takes that which belongs to Jesus, and transmits it to us! Hallelujah!

1 Samuel 2:8 "For the pillars of the earth are the LORD's,
And He has set the world upon them.
9 He will guard the feet of His saints,
But the wicked shall be silent in darkness.
"For by strength no man shall prevail.
10 The adversaries of the LORD shall be broken in pieces;
From heaven He will thunder against them.
The LORD will judge the ends of the earth.
"He will give strength to His king,
And exalt the horn of His anointed." NKJV

Thank you for taking the time to read this book on drawing from the anointing. With all my heart, I hope and pray that it will truly bless you and help empower you in your walk and in your ministry with our Lord and Savior Jesus Christ.

Amen

Printed in the United States
By Bookmasters